Struggling Learners:
Below Grade
or
Wrong Grade?

by
Jim Grant

MODERN LEARNING PRESS
ROSEMONT, NJ

ISBN 1-56762-176-7

Struggling Learners:
Below Grade or Wrong Grade?

Acknowledgments

I appreciate the fine work done by my editor, Robert Low, "the best friend a manuscript ever had" and a good friend of mine as well.

In addition to my family and Rob, I would also like to thank the following colleagues for their help and support over the years:
Char Forsten,
Betty Hollas,
Bob Johnson,
Jay LaRoche,
and Garry Myers.

The many other colleagues who have helped me along the way are too numerous to mention here. You know who you are, and you have my heartfelt thanks.

CONTENTS

INTRODUCTION

This new book evolved out of the first book I ever wrote. Much has changed since that first book began to take shape, but one critically important flaw in America's school systems has remained virtually unchanged:

Too many students end up struggling and failing because they are trapped in the wrong grade and need additional learning and growing time in order to succeed.

This is the "dirty little secret" of American education, and it remains the root cause of huge amounts of spending on remediation, summer school, and other forms of academic intervention that fail to solve the underlying problem. Even more important, it is the root cause of needless struggling and suffering by American children, anguish on the part of their parents, and deep concern among educators.

So much of this waste and pain can be eliminated if we only take a fair, common-sense approach to placing children in the correct grade and providing additional learning time when needed. And now that America's schools and educators are being held accountable for student performance and told to "leave no child behind," there may no longer be any alternative to doing the right thing for the children in our care.

The good news is that a relatively simple and inexpensive three-step solution can lead to dramatic and lasting improvements in many struggling learners' academic performance and quality of life. While the solution is faster and easier to summarize than to

i

implement, the following plan can have a profoundly positive effect without massive new investments and huge changes in American schools:

1. *Place children entering our school system in the correct grade, based on their individual needs and capabilities, rather than just counting birthday candles at some arbitrary "school entrance cut-off date."*

2. *If and when students start to struggle and fail after they have entered school, provide options that enable them to have an additional year of growing and learning time in a supportive, continuous-progress program.*

3. *To help prevent students from struggling and failing in any grade, use "differentiated instruction" to assess their needs and provide them with the educational materials and methods that are right for them.*

The remainder of this book explains why we need to do this and how we can succeed. Knowing that there's no time to waste when so many children are in need, let's proceed.

CHAPTER 1

Ready to Succeed, Set Up to Fail

"Everyone thinks I'm stupid."

"The teacher doesn't like me."

"I hate school!"

Every year, millions of young children walk into school for the first time, filled with excitement, fear, and high hopes. But by the end of their first school year, or in the years that follow, too many of these students will find themselves struggling, doing below-grade work, and failing—or at least feeling like failures. To be more accurate, the school system will fail many of its students, and their initial enthusiasm will turn into sadness and anger.

Over the years, students like these have been called a variety of names, including "slow," "lazy," "educationally handicapped," "unmotivated," "learning disabled," and "below grade level." Now, in an age of "zero tolerance" and "no excuses," these students are being told that they must succeed in meeting high grade-level standards each year, as documented by some test, no matter what name they have been called. Is it any wonder that these "severely labeled" students do not learn all they should—but do learn to dislike school and doubt themselves?

Their inability to meet grade-level standards has been blamed on everything from inadequate school funding to inadequate parent support, from a lack of discipline to a lack of stimulation, from low teacher salaries to low self-esteem. The list goes on and on. And while many experts waste time and energy debating where to assign the blame—or even whether the problem exists—too many of these students are way over their heads in school and continuing to sink further below grade level with each passing year.

Yet most of the students who are failing or just scraping by in school can succeed. Huge amounts of time, energy, and money are now being spent to help them get back up to the level at which they are "supposed" to be functioning. In some cases, these efforts will succeed, but in many other cases these efforts are doomed to fail, and the students they are intended to help will be doomed to fail, too, unless something different is done.

Why?

The answer is that many of these struggling students are not really below grade level. Instead, the truth of the matter is that they are actually placed one grade level *higher* than they should be, either because they were placed in the *wrong* grade when they first entered school, or because today's increasingly escalated, high-pressure, test-driven curriculum and methods of instruction have moved the "goalposts" out of range for a significant number of students, who might have been at grade level or above not so long ago. To better understand these two critically important causes and their widespread effects, let's take a moment to consider each.

Wrong grade placement has been around for a long time, but what's happening in America's schools today makes it more damaging and pervasive than ever before. Essentially, wrong grade placement occurs when all the children in a state or district are herded into a kindergarten program or grade solely on the basis of their age at some arbitrary "school entrance cut-off date." By relying solely on this sort of "cattle call," school officials and parents have ignored many vital developmental and educational factors that can and should be considered as part of the placement process. And the result is that many students have been unwittingly condemned to struggle and fail in the wrong grade. This is all the more tragic because so many of the children who will become struggling learners, below-grade students, or academic "failures" are intelligent and hard-working, and therefore could have succeeded in a grade for which they were truly ready.

Even as wrong grade placement continues to have a horrendous impact on a large number of students, today's sped-up, test-obsessed schools are creating even more struggling learners and below-grade students who end up in the wrong grade, even though they may have been placed in the correct grade initially. These students become "victims" of the system for many reasons, including the following:

- they are not good test takers (even though they are good students)
- they need a slower pace or different type of instruction (in order to learn successfully at their current grade level)
- they are not yet ready to comprehend and master more abstract concepts and skills that have recently been moved down from upper grades (and that they will be able to handle in the future)
- they are English as a Second Language (ESL) students (having grown up speaking and listening to a different language, they cannot comprehend as much written and oral information as other students, and they also are struggling with the added burden of learning an additional language)
- they are suffering from the effects of poverty and/or dysfunctional family situations (that interfere with their ability to learn and function well in school).

Many, if not all, of the struggling learners and below-grade students in these categories still can succeed in school. The students' individual needs and capabilities no longer match the standards, curriculum, instruction, and assessments being used in one particular grade, but may be a good match for the standards, curriculum, instruction, and assessments being used one grade lower. So rather than assuming that these students are simply not "measuring up" because of some intellectual/academic deficit or a bad attitude, the key to helping them achieve success is a simple three-step process of:

1. recognizing what they are ready to learn,
2. placing them in the right grade or program for their current needs and capabilities,
3. helping them proceed with appropriate instruction and support.

If, for example, a below-grade student can reasonably be expected to achieve success at his or her current grade level with an appropriate amount of academic intervention and other forms of support, then that is a solution worth trying for that particular student. But if other below-grade students were originally placed in the wrong grade or program and have continually had academic difficulties, or if they are now unable to succeed despite their best efforts, then school officials have a responsibility to correct the problem by placing those students where they can meet grade-level expectations. That is, placing them in the right grade or program—the one they are ready for.

The correct grade for a particular student might be a different grade than the one that many of his or her chronological peers are in, or it might be a multiage classroom in which several grades are blended together, or it might be a "transition" class that provides an additional year of continuous-progress education between two grades. These and other options will be explored in greater detail later in this book. But no matter which option is used, the basic premise remains the same: students should not and cannot be allowed to struggle and fail simply because of an initially incorrect or now-obsolete grade placement decision. Instead, the educators and parents responsible for the student's education need to determine what and how the student is ready to learn, and then place the student in the grade or program where he or she can learn successfully.

The success of this approach—and the need for it—are well documented, because students' lack of readiness for their current grade or program has been a long-standing and widespread problem in American schools. Nationwide surveys of elementary school teachers at the start of the new millennium reported results similar to those from a decade earlier, finding that close to 40% of the students were not ready for the grade or program in which they had been placed. And the emphasis on setting high grade-level standards has made many grades or programs even more difficult since then, even though there has not been a corresponding increase in students' readiness and ability to succeed. In fact, the lack of readiness documented below has remained remarkably consistent with the findings of researchers going back to the 1960s and 1970s.

"The results of this survey mirror national reports stating that 40 percent of children entering the school system are not prepared."
– Doug Price, founder of Educare Colorado and sponsor of a survey of 1,000 Colorado kindergarten and first grade teachers, as quoted in *Education Week*, March 6, 2002.

"Students are not fully prepared to learn at their grade level...55% of teachers report that all, most or at least more than one-quarter of their students are unprepared...It should be noted that lack of preparedness is a problem at all grade levels."
– 1992 Metropolitan Life Survey of the American Teacher.

"Frankly, we found it deeply troubling, ominous really that 35% of the nation's children—more than one in three—are not ready for school, according to the teachers. Even more disturbing, when we asked how the readiness of last year's

students compared to those who enrolled five years ago, 42 percent of the respondents said the situation is getting worse; only 25 percent said it's better."
– Ernest Boyer, *Ready to Learn*, citing a 1991 survey conducted by The Carnegie Foundation for the Advancement of Teaching.

During the 1990s, efforts were made to address this problem by reforming the elementary school curriculum and establishing a "readiness goal"—that by the year 2000, all children would start school ready to learn and succeed. The plan for reaching this goal, however, required extensive changes in the nation's health care system, Head Start programs, and public schools, along with massive amounts of spending. Of course, many of these changes and spending increases never occurred, and now that the new millennium has arrived, very little is being said about the readiness goal or the fact that our country did not even come close to reaching it. Meanwhile, too many of America's children continue to find themselves struggling and failing in grades for which they are not ready.

In previous decades and in the current one, parents and teachers have often misread the plight of these students. Too many students being failed by their schools have been assigned the blame for the problem. Once described as "not very bright," "not really trying," or "not living up to their potential," today these students may be suspected of having an attention deficit disorder or learning disability, especially as more advanced material is pushed down into lower grades and the tempo of instruction is quickened. In fact, many bright, motivated, high-potential students with a normal attention span and cognitive abilities actually become "curriculum-disabled" because they are trapped in the wrong grade or program.

Some of these children are developing at a different (yet normal) rate compared to many of their peers. Through no fault of their own, their bodies, minds, and emotions have not yet reached the stage required for success in a particular grade or program. These "developmentally young" children are also called "late bloomers" —students who can reach their full (and often extraordinary) potential when schools provide the additional learning and growing time they need. Other students may have reached the appropriate developmental stage for a grade, but because of the students' individual needs—or because the curriculum and methods of instruction have become too advanced or otherwise inappropriate—these students are truly incapable of doing grade-level work.

In the course of your life, you probably have known students like these, and you may even have been such a student yourself. There is hardly a person alive in the United States who has not had someone in his family scarred by the experience of failure or marginal performance in school. The anonymous statements at the beginning of this chapter will sound all too familiar to any educator or parent who has experienced firsthand the misery of a struggling learner in the wrong grade.

These students are just too plentiful to avoid or ignore. And especially now that large numbers of these students are being told that they, their teachers, and their schools are all failures because the students cannot meet grade-level standards, we have a responsibility to identify the real causes of the problem and then implement effective solutions. Otherwise, today's efforts to hold schools and educators "accountable" will actually do terrible damage to large numbers of students, and the resulting anger and despair will lead to demands that those who created and implemented these education policies be held accountable for the consequences of their acts.

"The Louisiana state board of elementary and secondary education adopted a policy of nonpromotion of students who fail either the mathematics or English portion of the [Louisiana Educational Assessment Program] test. During the 2000-01 school year, some 18,000 Louisiana students were denied promotion

7

based on their performance on the test, according to court documents."
– *Education Week* article from March 6, 2002, reporting that the U.S. Supreme Court declined to hear a case about the linkage of high-stakes testing and grade-level promotion.

Grade placement done right

Too often, school entrance and grade placement decisions fail to take into account vital differences in chronological ages, developmental stages, gender, and other factors, as well as the individual needs of a specific student. Yet these differences can and frequently do determine whether the student ends up at grade level, above grade level, below grade level—or in the wrong grade altogether. A few brief questions and answers should therefore always be considered when evaluating a child's initial educational placement and subsequent grade assignments.

Has the child started school at the "right" age?

In nearly all states, the primary means of evaluating a child's readiness for school is counting the number of birthday candles at a particular "cut-off" date. The cut-off dates vary widely from state to state, so that a child in one state who turns 5 in August may not be allowed to start kindergarten until another year has gone by, while just across the state line a child who will turn 5 in November may be required to start kindergarten in September, even though he will still be only 4 years old at that time. In most states, these cut-off dates were arbitrarily set years or even decades ago, and so are totally unrelated to the type of curriculum and the difficulty of the state's current grade-level standards.

Obviously, this simplistic, old-fashioned, and illogical approach is just not fair to children who are ready for different educational experiences. When you are 5 years old, six months represents about one-tenth of the total time you have been alive. A tremendous amount of development takes place during this sort of time span. Nevertheless, in any single grade at most schools, there are students as much as twelve months younger than their classmates.

Studies done by Dr. James Uphoff and other researchers have shown that the younger students in a grade are far more likely to experience serious problems in school than older students in the same grade. And Dr. Uphoff has found that this pattern continues all the way through high school—and beyond.

"The chronologically younger children in any grade are far more likely than the older children in that grade to:
- *earn lower grades*
- *score lower on achievement tests*
- *be diagnosed as Learning Disabled*
- *be in special service programs such as Title I*
- *be less attentive in class*
- *be behind their grade peers in athletic skill level*
- *be chosen less frequently for leadership roles by peers or adults*
- *have failed a grade*
- *become dropouts*
- *rank lower in their graduating class*
- *be a suicide victim."*

– Dr. James Uphoff, Ed.D., *Real Facts from Real Schools: What You're Not Supposed to Know about School Readiness & Transition Programs.*

Is the student in the right grade or program at the right time?

As noted earlier, students do not all develop at the exact same rate. Each child has an internal time clock that determines personal growth and development in the emotional, social, physical, and intellectual spheres. While other factors also affect a child's development and academic performance, the current stage and rate of development have a powerful impact on the child's ability to meet grade-level expectations or requirements. Yet many schools (and state standards) treat students as if they are all at the same developmental stage and are continuing to develop at the same rate, even though numerous studies have shown that there is a wide variation among children's stages and rates of development at any particular time.

For example, among 6-year-old children you will notice a very wide range in height, weight, personality, language use, and ability to perform tasks. The variations are linked, at least in part, to the rate at which these students are developing and maturing. But in many schools each first grader is now expected to meet the same state standards as every other first grader, and do it in the exact same time span—180 days.

During the 1990s, some "experts" who acknowledged children's developmental differences still claimed that only one single program was needed at each grade level, because teachers could simply "individualize" the curriculum and instruction to meet the diverse needs of all the students in a class. In reality, even when the curriculum was "developmentally appropriate," some students could not accomplish or learn all that was needed within a typical 180-day time frame, no matter how much the teacher tried to meet individual needs. Since then, the increasing diversity of America's student population, when combined with required adherence to rigid state standards and the pressure to prepare students for state tests, has made effectively "individualizing" the curriculum and instruction an impossibility for many teachers. Moreover, these same state standards and tests have forced many elementary school programs to adopt an advanced academic curriculum that is not in sync with the developmental needs of numerous students.

So what is going to happen to the students who are developmentally and/or chronologically younger than most of their peers? As early as kindergarten, these children, who may actually be intellectually superior, are going to have difficulty with the curriculum and start falling behind. Then, their inability to master needed information and skills will make the next grade even more stressful and increase the likelihood that they will do below-grade work. It may also lead to negative feelings about themselves and their school, which in turn will contribute to even poorer performance.

This "vicious cycle" is then likely to continue and even accelerate the rate and extent to which the students fall below grade level. The alternative and solution, of course, is to provide the additional learning and growing time the student needs—by putting the student into the grade for which the student is actually ready.

Is the child a boy or a girl?

Anyone who has ever visited an elementary school classroom has undoubtedly observed that boys generally have a much harder time there than girls do. The reason is that girls generally mature at a faster rate than boys. By the age of 6, girls are—on average—six months ahead of boys in their development. As children grow older, the gap widens. That's why tenth grade girls like to date twelfth grade boys, and why twelfth grade girls like to date college freshmen. Most experts believe that males catch up with females in early adulthood, although some people question whether males ever catch up.

Back in kindergarten and the elementary grades, the discrepancy in development between boys and girls makes an enormous difference. As pointed out earlier, six months or a year represents a large percentage of the total life span of a 5- or 6-year-old. In addition, as Dr. Anthony Coletta points out in his book, *What's Best for Kids*, young girls tend to have an advantage over young boys in fine-motor skills such as writing and drawing, while young males are typically better at gross-motor skills such as throwing and catching. The fine-motor system is closely related to the development of language and the ability to read, giving many girls an early advantage in reading, spelling, talking, and listening.

Under these circumstances, guess how a girl and a boy born on the same day will fare in many elementary schools. The girl is likely to make good progress in learning to read and write, enjoy school, and develop confidence in her abilities. The boy is likely to have more trouble sitting still and learning to read and write.

He is less likely to enjoy school and develop confidence in his ability to learn and do well in school. He may even be suspected of having an attention deficit disorder, when all he really needs is some additional time to develop and learn.

"Boys are expected to do too much too soon—their brains aren't ready for it...I've come to the conclusion that later enrollment would solve 80 percent of the problems we see with boys and school today."
– Leonard Sax, family physician and psychologist, quoted in *U.S. News & World Report*, July 30, 2001.

Are there other factors or circumstances that may be affecting the child's readiness for and performance in school?

In order to learn in school, students need to be able to focus their attention and listen well—tasks that are much more difficult when a student is also experiencing physical or social/emotional problems. Parents and teachers therefore should consider a wide range of factors that can have a serious impact on a student's ability to do grade-level work.

Physically, students need to start each day with a good breakfast, so they have sufficient energy and are not distracted by hunger pangs during the day. They should also have had a good night's sleep, so they are not struggling to stay awake and focus their attention. Students' vision and hearing ability should be checked frequently, especially if they are having problems in school or are experiencing headaches, earaches, or allergies.

Other current or previous experiences that may also affect a student's physical readiness include prenatal or postnatal exposure to drugs or environmental toxins (including tobacco), prematurity, low birth weight, poor nutrition, and serious or extended illnesses.

Emotionally, children find it easier to learn when they are not coping with the death of someone important to them, relocation to a new home, separation from one or both parents, or the birth of a sibling. Other sources of emotional stress that can affect children's ability to learn include violence in the home or the community, substance abuse by a parent, the incarceration of a parent, and various forms of child abuse or neglect.

Moreover, experienced educators recognize that some students are being forced to cope not just with one of the problems cited above, but with "multiple co-occurring factors and circumstances" that make achieving success in school far more difficult and complicated. And not surprisingly, children growing up in poverty are more likely to experience this sort of combination of problems, with the predictable effect on their learning and performance in school.

"Just 67 percent of 1st graders from impoverished families were able to recognize words by sight, for example, compared with 86 percent of 1st graders from families that were not poor, the study found. Children living in poverty were also less likely than those from higher-income families to be adding and subtracting by late in the 1st grade—60 percent, compared with 79 percent."
– Data from the Early Childhood Longitudinal Study, as reported in the March 20, 2002 issue of *Education Week*.

What are the individual needs of this particular child?

A child's overall emotional disposition—independent of any external factors—is also worth considering. Students who are temperamentally difficult or shy are likely to find a new grade or program more challenging and stressful than a confidant, outgoing child who adapts easily to new situations. And rather than helping shy or difficult children overcome their temperaments, feeling trapped in the wrong grade tends to reinforce such children's negative expectations, creating new obstacles that must also be overcome.

In evaluating a student's readiness for and placement in a grade, parents and teachers need to consider the unique combination of characteristics which make up the "whole" child, rather than focusing on just one aspect. For example, the fact that a child was born in August does not automatically mean that he or she is unready for a particular grade or program. But a shy, left-handed boy who was born in August, then had a serious illness, and recently moved to town is less likely to be ready than an outgoing, right-handed girl who was born in the same month but has since had a very healthy childhood and lived in the same house.

A parent's understanding of a child and an educator's understanding of the grade or program the child will be participating in are the key criteria for evaluating a child's educational readiness and performance. This deep, firsthand knowledge is far more important than the statistical data cited in media stories or ivory tower debates. One reason is that some statistics have been manipulated by researchers trying to prove a point. More important, what is right for some or even many children may still be wrong for the particular child under discussion. Children are unique individuals, after all, not norms or percentages.

Can you make sure a child is ready for a particular grade or program?

Can you make a child grow an extra twelve inches by this time next year? Of course not. Nor can you appreciably speed up the rate at which a child matures emotionally, socially, physically, or intellectually. What you can do is make sure that a child's readiness is evaluated and considered, and then find the option that best meets the child's needs.

Before or when a child enters a primary grade or program, a fairly simple readiness assessment can provide valuable information about the child's stage of development. (More information about readiness assessments can be found in Chapter 5.) This information, when combined with parental input and the observations of educators, can lead to a placement decision that matches the child to the curriculum most appropriate for that child, thereby providing the best opportunity to achieve success in school.

Children who are not developmentally ready for one grade or program need to have the option of participating in a grade or program that is appropriate for them. This is why many schools have a "readiness" program that provides a year of developmentally appropriate education before kindergarten, as well as "transition" classes that provide an additional year of continuous-progress education after kindergarten. In school districts where such programs are not available, parents of a child who needs an additional year may want to have their child attend an extra year of preschool. (These sorts of options are discussed in more detail in Chapter 6.)

In the upper grades, a student's *continued* inability to meet grade-level standards, even after sustained academic intervention, is a strong indication that the student is not ready for the next grade level. While good students sometimes have a bad year, many students originally placed in the wrong grade have a clear pattern of struggle and failure that goes right back to kindergarten. Other students may have started out well but gradually or suddenly began falling behind, until they are almost—or even more than—a full year behind. Unfortunately, once students reach this point, it is unlikely they will be able to make up such a large deficit while remaining in the same grade.

As the underlying problem for these sorts of students is that they are now in a grade one year ahead of where they should be, the fairest, most appropriate, and most effective intervention is to provide a full additional year of learning time, either in an upper-grade transition program or by taking an additional year to complete their current grade. (The latter option is discussed in more detail in Chapter 7.)

What if a student's performance is below grade level but the student is unwilling or unable to obtain an additional year of learning time?

If the student's problems are purely academic and not too severe, then effective academic intervention coupled with smaller amounts of additional learning time may solve the problems. Specialists can provide valuable support in the classroom or through pull-out programs, while after-school programs, tutoring, and summer school can also help students catch up—if they are not too far below grade level. (Chapter 8 provides suggestions for helping students improve below-grade work while remaining in the same grade.)

However, if the student's problems are *not* simply academic, then academic intervention cannot solve the underlying problem. And if the student is a full year behind, smaller amounts of additional learning time will not be enough to bridge the gap, especially when there has been a history of struggle and failure that has resulted in negative attitudes and expectations.

Why is Jim Grant so sure that additional learning time can make the difference between school success and failure?

I have seen it happen too many times during my decades of experience as a teacher, principal, and education consultant. And I have found that my own professional development parallels that of most other educators, who have come to the same conclusions.

When I was the young teacher of a class filled with a typically diverse group of students, I knew that something was drastically wrong. Unfortunately, I did not have the background knowledge needed to identify the problem, much less find the solution. Nothing in my previous training had prepared me for the situation I faced every single day in that classroom. At that time (and even today), few teacher-training institutes provided information about child development and readiness. So like many other educators, I blamed the students, the textbooks, the parents, and my own inadequacy for the fact that the students' needs were not being met.

Fortunately, when I became the principal of the entire school, I had just enough sense to know that I needed the problem-solving skills of an expert. I turned to Nancy Richard, a child development specialist who had secured a Title III (federal) grant used to create readiness programs in schools throughout New Hampshire. (Nancy also happened to have taught me when I was in high school.) With her help, I began to observe the wide range of developmental levels among the students within the classes. I could then see clearly that many students were not well matched with the curriculum and were unable to complete it successfully in the fixed amount of time available.

In attempting to correct this situation, I first tried working with teachers to individualize their programs to meet the needs of each child. This helped some students, but there were others who simply were not ready for the demands of the grade to which they were assigned. It was only when the school began providing these students with appropriate amounts of additional learning time that they began to experience their rightful success. In other words, rather than trying (and failing) to make children ready for school, the school truly became ready for its students.

This experience pointed me in an educational direction that has changed my career and my life, as well as the lives of many students who attended my school and other schools I have worked with. The simple but profound concept of readiness is the fundamental issue for many students who are struggling and failing in school. And providing these students with additional learning time is an absolute necessity in order for them to achieve school success.

17

Meeting the real needs of struggling learners

Most teachers and parents know when something is wrong with a student's educational experience. And most will do whatever they can to correct it. If you could make an appropriate, legal, and widely used change that would enable a frustrated, struggling student to start learning happily and successfully, wouldn't you do it? Of course you would. The needs of the children in your care are your paramount concern, and you know their future will depend to a large extent on the type of experiences they have in school.

Placing a student in the right grade or program is exactly the sort of change that can and must be made for many struggling learners. And making that change is more important than ever, now that the federal government and states across the country have established high standards and are using high-stakes tests to ensure that all students meet those standards before proceeding to a new grade level. This approach has raised the possibility that each struggling student will be required to spend an additional year in an upper grade after struggling for too long to meet grade-level standards and then finally failing a high-stakes test.

Establishing standards and requiring accountability are valid and even essential aspects of school reform, but waiting until a student fails—and relying solely on test scores to determine failure—will result in a lot of unnecessary damage being done. When this occurs, much of the additional learning time must be spent trying to make up for educational deficits and helping to overcome the bad habits and bad attitudes that so often develop when students struggle and remain below grade level for many years.

Consider instead how much more positive and effective an additional year of learning time would be if students received it before they had spent much of their young lives struggling and failing to master the curriculum. The concept of "early intervention" is now

18

widely accepted as an effective, proactive approach to academic support, because it solves problems as soon as they become apparent rather than allowing them to grow worse. In a similar way, a proactive approach to additional learning time is also needed to solve the underlying problem of many struggling students.

Today we know enough about how children develop and learn to give each child the proper start in school—or, if the child is already in school, to place the child in the right grade. By doing so, we can help far more students achieve success in school, rather than allowing so many of them to become trapped in a downward spiral of struggle and failure. But before we focus on the solution, let's make sure we fully understand the problem.

CHAPTER 2

Learning to Be a Success—or a Failure

"Unready children are trapped in a situation where they are humiliated in front of their friends every day, and survival becomes a matter of escape by daydreaming...clowning...avoiding school...developing psychosomatic illnesses..."
–Nancy Richard, education consultant.

I still vividly remember my elementary school years. I bet you re-member yours, too—those childhood experiences are etched into our brains, unless they were so painful they have been blotted out of conscious memory.

In 1948 the school door opened and children flooded in. Other than chronological age and a heartbeat, there were virtually no entrance or placement criteria. If you were 5, you were ready for kindergarten. If you were 6, you were ready for first grade. And so on and so on, or so everyone thought.

The only exceptions were the physically and mentally handi-capped, who had no federally legislated programs to protect them back then. Once these sorts of children were identified as "re-jects," they were sent back home or in some cases allowed to "pass time" in school until they were old enough to drop out.

The remaining children were divided up into three basic "tracks."

The low achievers experienced firsthand what it's like to live at the bottom of a caste system. They ended up in the "Buzzard" class or reading group, from which came most of the future drop-outs, kids with behavior problems, and users of remedial services. In too many cases, this happened just because these students were not ready for their grade or program placement.

The average achievers, identified by their scores on a reading readiness test, were designated "Bluebirds." Though some were intellectually superior but developmentally young, the "average" label clung to them like a burr throughout their school careers.

The teacher's delight were the top scorers on the reading readiness test, students proudly assigned to the "Peacock" reading group. Academic learning came easily for them, but some paid a price in terms of their social and emotional growth.

A few fluent readers—the "gifted and talented"—were moved onto the fast track. Subject to the perils of acceleration, many of these children who skipped over a grade had an important developmental cycle excised from their lives. Usually they made it up later—some by coasting through high school or dropping out of college, and many by taking a year off in some other way.

More than intelligence goes to school

Back then, educators not only acted as though chronological age was the only criterion for entrance and placement decisions, they also grouped children within a grade or class according to one single criterion—the intellect. Academic achievement was all-important; students' emotional, social, and physical needs were ignored.

The tracking of young children in this way failed to take into account the damage that labeling and grouping can have on children's self-image, attitudes toward school, and academic performance. Fortunately, most educators now recognize that more than a child's intellect goes to school, and that tracking is flawed even in regard to intellectual capabilities. The use of standardized test scores as a basis for tracking young students is now widely acknowledged to be unreliable as well as harmful.

Academically, the long-term danger is that tracking tends to become a "self-fulfilling prophecy," as most children know very well which group they have been placed in—no matter what it is called. Kids placed in a "dummy" class may simply assume that the adults' evaluation of them is correct, giving them little reason to try hard and a very good excuse for remaining below grade level. This is bad enough when the students in the class truly have a limited capacity for learning, but when the class also includes students who are actually bright but trapped in the wrong grade, it is a terribly unfair waste.

"As students pass the years organized in ways that separate them, they become polarized into pro- and anti-school camps that become increasingly estranged from one another (Gamoran and Berends 1987, p.426). One group achieves success in the classroom; the other finds success in the hallways and playgrounds."
–Paul George, *How to Untrack Your School*

In many of today's classrooms, teachers use flexible grouping policies in an effort to avoid tracking, labeling, and stigmatizing students unfairly. The students all learn together during whole-class lessons and activities, after which the class may be broken down into smaller groups for short periods of time. In some cases, the achievement levels within the groups may also be mixed, with cooperative learning or "differentiated" projects being used to provide appropriate learning experiences for the full range of students. In other cases, the groups are organized by achievement level, so that, for example, students ready to work with multiplication or chapter books don't have to waste their time on lessons about addition and story books.

While a variety of imaginative euphemisms have been developed to identify the different levels of learners, the basic categories still boil down to advanced, average, and below average. And no matter which approach and terms are used, the individual students still know what level of work they are capable of doing. They also know (or think they know) who the smart kids and the dumb kids are.

As a result, students who are developmentally or chronologically young tend to think they are dumb, because they always seem less capable than the rest of the class and need extra help. Other students who are developmentally or chronologically older—but still unable to thrive in a fast-paced, memorization-based, skill-drilled curriculum—are likely to reach similar conclusions about themselves. Struggling learners trapped in this situation will continue striving to live up to their potential (for a while), but many grow increasingly frustrated and alienated, until they finally decide that clinging to hope and making the extra effort are no longer worthwhile because the end result is only more disappointment and failure.

Another common practice in schools today can also contribute to the negative attitudes struggling learners have about school and themselves, even though this practice can and often does provide effective assistance. In many schools, children whose performance is below grade level may be "pulled out" of class to work with a reading specialist, a speech therapist, or a resource teacher. In other schools, the specialist may "push in" to work with a particular group of kids in one part of the classroom, while the (regular) teacher continues the (regular) school work with the (regular) students.

Most educators work hard and successfully to diminish or even eliminate any stigma attached to being part of a group that works with a specialist. And students who receive effective intervention and support can then "graduate" from their groups and go on to become strong and successful students. But other students remain in one—or several—of these groups year after year. Meanwhile, these students know why they are in the groups, know how their performance compares with that of other students, and know that all the other students know exactly who is in which group.

When the students working with specialists are actually late bloomers or other struggling learners trapped in a grade higher than the one they are actually ready for, then all the extra effort and expense intended to get these students "up" to grade level cannot really solve the underlying problem. And if the students later happen to fail a high-stakes test required for passage to a new grade level, the negative image they have of themselves will be confirmed. At that point, having been publicly designated a failure and forced to repeat a grade, they will finally receive the additional year of learning and growing time they actually needed long before. Unfortunately, it is unlikely to do as much good as it would have done a few years earlier.

Labels can last a lifetime

Providing the additional learning time sooner rather than later is preferable because students who are grouped, officially labeled, or have categorized themselves during their elementary school years often internalize these images and carry them inside long after they have entered the adult world. Young children, in particular, are just beginning to develop a self-image through their interaction with classmates and teachers, so they are particularly susceptible to others' evaluation of them.

Moreover, children, not unlike adults, do not easily forget humiliation and embarrassment. With their antennae attuned to the people they depend on and admire, children are quick to perceive the disappointment felt by adults in their world. This is particularly true of students trapped in grades or programs for which they are not ready, who are then grouped or labeled in ways that indicate they are not coping successfully. These students tend to accumulate feelings of anxiety, inadequacy, and self-doubt with surprising speed.

These feelings are reinforced when a student hears his or her name frequently mentioned by the teacher in a negative or nagging tone. Even worse, the student may hear frequent renditions of the same old theme: "You can do better if you really try." Usually the student really is trying, if he or she hasn't already given up, but effort alone is not enough to overcome the disadvantage of being mismatched with a wrong grade's curriculum and methods of instruction.

In another misguided attempt to spur a student on, a teacher may further damage the student's self-esteem by comparing that student with another. Or a parent may do similar damage by comparing the child to a "successful" brother or sister. All too often, a child put in this situation sees the emphasis as being on the contrast between the two—the differences rather than the similarities—and therefore assumes that he or she must be a "failure" if the other one is a "success."

A child can endure such a barrage of negative feedback for just so long before feeling defective as a person. The child is inclined to love and trust his parents and teachers, so when he or she cannot please these significant adults, the response is likely to be, "There must be something wrong with me." And now that high grade-level standards are the basis for evaluating students in schools across America, a student who struggles and fails to meet those standards is quite likely to feel "substandard," even if the fault really lies with the adults who placed and kept the student in the wrong grade.

The student's feelings of inadequacy and failure may be further reinforced when parents and teachers collaborate on additional ways to improve the student's below-grade performance. Summer school, before- and after-school programs, Saturday sessions, private tutoring, counseling—all these well-intentioned efforts to help the student may actually do further harm. While they often result in some specific but limited improvement in school performance, they may also become further confirmation of the student's personal inadequacy and unworthiness, especially if they end up being futile efforts that cannot provide what the student truly needs—a full additional year to develop and learn.

"In reality, a group of young children cannot all succeed when pressed to learn 'on schedule.' It is unrealistic and unfair to assume all the students in the same class will master the same concept or skill at the same time. They need to be allowed to acquire skills at their own individual pace."
–Anthony Coletta, Ph.D., *What's Best for Kids.*

Similar negative feelings tend to develop when a student is "socially promoted" year after year without having successfully completed the curriculum for each grade. Due to financial pressures and an ideological smear campaign that claimed any additional year of learning time is "grade-level retention" and therefore bad, some parents and educators still believe that simply passing the student along from grade to grade is best for the child. However, the student, his or her classmates, and the teacher all know that the student cannot perform at the same level as most of the other students. And by failing to learn the needed information and skills that then become the foundation for success in higher grade levels, he or she is likely to keep falling further below grade level.

This knowledge—and the patterns it creates—eat away at the student's self-esteem, actual learning, and attitude toward school. Meanwhile, year after year there remains a vague and increasingly futile hope that at some magic moment the student will suddenly "catch up." Instead, it is now far more likely that the emphasis on high standards and high-stakes testing will finally "catch up" with the student, whose quiet, daily failure in the classroom will finally be broadcast to all when passage to a higher grade is refused.

Failure on the installment plan

These sorts of negative and unfair experiences can inhibit a student from trying and succeeding in school. One teacher described the burden carried by a student in the wrong grade or program as an "emotional mortgage." Unfortunately, this sort of mortgage may never be paid off, because the negative experiences create expectations and patterns of behavior that compound themselves like unpaid interest—and often prove difficult, if not impossible, to work off.

Some students, for example, exhibit what psychologists call "avoidance behavior," a fancy term for what most of us know as plain old procrastination. Students who rely on procrastination as a survival technique—avoiding work, avoiding encounters, avoiding any kind of conflict or challenge—often continue this habit as adults, thereby missing many opportunities for happiness and success.

Other patterns that become ingrained in students due to years of struggle and stress in school include:
- fear of taking risks
- nervousness
- oversensitivity
- lack of confidence
- lack of ease in social situations
- aggressiveness
- making excuses.

In recent years, the terms used to describe these behaviors may have changed to *anxiety, withdrawal, depression,* and *antisocial behavior.* Also, medications are now frequently prescribed to lessen the symptoms, but the patterns and underlying causes remain very much the same.

An adult who suffered and failed in school as a young child, and the parents of others like him, testify to the long-term negative effects of this experience:

"...how lonely I was. I was always too immature, both physically and emotionally, for the group I was with. Many of my social, personal, and even professional failures in adult life I lay to the fact that I went too fast, much too fast, all the way through school."

"My oldest son...started first grade when he was several months short of 6 years old...[The result was] years of constant struggle, inadequacy, frustration, and discouragement [which] finally caught up with Derrick in his junior and senior high school years...He is very self-deprecating and miserable...Here was a youngster of better-than-average intelligence...with a driving desire to measure up...crushed by twelve school years."

"...it took Tim years to recover from the pain he experienced in his first two years of school. Ten years later, he still has trouble when he is presented with a new task or problem."

Ready for what?

The public school system that is educating children today has probably changed greatly in many respects since you and I were in school, but it may not have changed at all in regard to its basic structure. Chances are you started kindergarten at age 5 and were then expected to move through the grades in lockstep with other students your age. Then:

- A certain percentage of the students (perhaps including yourself) failed to complete the coursework in time and were forced to repeat a grade.

- Others (perhaps including yourself) barely scraped by and learned relatively little but were passed along from grade to grade, until finally graduating with a huge sigh of relief.
- A third group (perhaps including yourself) mastered the curriculum each and every year and came back ready for more, then went on to college feeling the same way.

Rather than forcing all these different types of students to master the same curriculum in the exact same amount of time—or else be deemed a failure—many schools now offer an additional year of learning time in proactive ways that meet the needs of a wide range of students. As noted earlier, these supportive and effective options may include a "readiness" year before kindergarten, a "transition" class between two grades, or a "multiage" class in which students can remain one additional year. Through options such as these, students can learn and grow successfully in a positive, continuous-progress environment. They also can avoid being trapped by artificial distinctions such as grade levels and cut-off dates that may not be well matched to the difficulty of the curriculum, state standards, and related tests, much less to the individual student's current stage and rate of development.

"Our timebound mentality has forced us into believing that schools can educate all of the people all of the time in a school year of 180 six-hour days. The consequence of our self-deception has been to ask the impossible of our students."
–Report of the National Commission on Time and Learning, 1994.

By providing a variety of educational options, contemporary educators recognize that virtually every student is ready to learn, wants to learn, and can learn, as long as the material and teaching methods are appropriate for the student's developmental stage and intellectual capabilities. Providing these options also recognizes the importance of early intervention in helping students master needed information and skills, as well as in developing positive attitudes about learning and themselves, so they can achieve their full potential as students and as adults. And these options provide a vital form of school choice—within a single school.

Do these concepts of developmental readiness and providing an additional year of learning time run counter to your personal history—to impressions you formed when you were young about the way school is supposed to be? If so, this may make it difficult for you to accept what has become an essential and proven solution for many struggling students. And with all the talk these days about the need for competitive advantages, as well as all the pressure on teachers to have their students "measure up" on state tests, you may feel you need to push students as hard and as quickly as possible.

In particular, recent trends and policies have reintroduced the idea that the earlier children are introduced to academic subjects, the more successful the children will be. However, the opposite is often the case.

Childhood should be a journey, not a race

Many children learn and grow better when adults resist the current fashion to hurry them—to speed up their exposure to new concepts and experiences in an effort to help them get ahead of others. Extensive research and the experiences of many educators have shown that students need to progress through a particular stage of development at their own rate in order to complete the tasks of the next stage successfully.

For example, young children who "play" with crayons, picture books, blocks, water, sand, and other hands-on objects are actually learning the rudiments of writing, reading, mathematics, physics, and other disciplines in an age-appropriate way. This prepares them to succeed with more abstract concepts like words and numbers when they are physically and mentally ready to work with abstractions. If children are pressured to memorize letters and numbers before they are developmentally ready, they lack the deeper understanding of the concepts behind these symbols and cannot work with them effectively.

Yet today's parents are being told:

How to Teach Your Baby to Read,
How to Give Your Baby Encyclopedic Knowledge,
How to Multiply Your Baby's Intelligence,
How to Raise a Brighter Child,
Kindergarten Is Too Late.

You might think I invented these phrases to ridicule what's happening today, but these are actual titles of books published for parents. And now there's even computer software that offers to help you "jump start" your baby or toddler. Products and concepts like these are featured on television and radio and in the print media, where a weekly news magazine talks about "Bringing Up Super Baby" and a front-page newspaper photo shows 5-year-olds in caps and gowns on "Kindergarten Graduation Day."

Were any pseudo-experts able to make your baby girl walk before her muscles were ready to support her? Can they now accelerate the rate at which your son loses his baby teeth and replaces them with their successors? Not a chance. Yet these rush-'em-into-reading experts claim they can turn your baby into a crawling encyclopedia and that letting children progress at their natural rate is a big mistake.

This sort of hurry-up hype is depriving children of their childhood. Not only is it detrimental to their mental and physical health, it may actually lead to long-term problems that prevent children from learning when and how they should.

"…many parents and even some teachers have unknowingly blocked progression through the stages of learning to read, by introducing phonics before children have demonstrated the ability to memorize and retell stories, as well as understand concepts about print."
–Anthony Coletta, Ph.D., *What's Best for Kids*

It is a terrible irony that some well-intentioned adults have actually set up children to fail before the children even started kindergarten. And other parents and educators make similar mistakes once children have entered preschool or elementary school, by not allowing children to take the time they need to develop and succeed.

The tortoise and the hare

As children, many of us read the classic fable about the race between the tortoise and the hare. The hare sprinted far ahead early on, but it eventually became so tired and uninterested it lost the race to the tortoise, which proceeded at the steady pace that matched its capabilities. Knowing today's high-pressure, test-driven schools, let's consider what might happen to the tortoise and the hare early in a race held at such a school:

The tortoise would probably be suspected of having developmental delays or hidden disabilities, while the hare would be celebrated as a role model.

The tortoise might be "pulled out" of class to work with a running specialist, while the hare would be designated a "gifted and talented" sprinter.

The tortoise might also be required to work with a tutor after school and on weekends, while the hare would be allowed to rest up, enjoy life, and pursue other interests.

The tortoise would probably be pressured to change its rate and pace of progress, while the hare would be allowed to "coast" because it was already so far ahead of the competition.

The tortoise would probably receive poor results on an interim assessment and therefore be considered a struggling, below-grade runner, while the hare's early success would be perceived as validating the techniques and strategies used by its trainers.

The truth, of course, is the same today as it was hundreds of years ago, when the fable of the tortoise and the hare first became popular. Experienced parents and educators have seen too many little "superstars" burn out when they reached the upper grades, because being pushed too hard to do too much too soon left these students with little enthusiasm for and interest in learning. Meanwhile, other students—who got off to a slow start but received the additional time and support they needed—became committed and successful learners whose achievements were at or above grade level in high school and beyond.

The following chapter provides a more detailed look at what happens to a student's education when these important lessons are ignored.

CHAPTER 3

Rob's Story: "In the right grade, he's above grade level."

o·ver·place (oh-ver-plays) *verb* 1. To assign a child to a wrong grade or program, which is too advanced and therefore inappropriate for the child's developmental or academic level, putting the child at risk for below-grade performance and school failure as well as harmful stress.

Welcome to kindergarten

Because his birthday is August 19th, Robert Eagen started school when he had just turned 5 years old. Where Rob lives, a child must be 5 by September 1st to enter kindergarten. Mr. and Mrs. Eagen were pleased that their son was not excluded by the cut-off date and that he had scored well on the cognitive examination administered to all incoming kindergarten students. They were proud of their boy, and he was excited, although a little nervous, about starting school.

On the first day of class, Rob clung to his mother when she started to leave. But with a lot of coaxing, he was finally persuaded to stay. By the middle of the first week of kindergarten, however, he began to cry and have stomachaches in the morning. Getting him off to school was a battle.

The Eagen family had gone through a similar experience when Rob started preschool. Mr. and Mrs. Eagen had chosen a preschool that used a developmental approach, with an emphasis on building social skills and learning through play. Even so, Rob initially hadn't wanted his mother to leave, but once he grew used to the routine and made some friends, he was willing to stay there by himself. In the relaxed, supportive atmosphere, Rob eventually seemed happy and did well. The preschool teachers assured Mr. and Mrs. Eagen that Rob was an intelligent young boy who would also do well in elementary school.

Based on this experience, Rob's father and mother insisted that he go to kindergarten every day. They were sure they knew what was best for their son and that he would "grow out" of his current problems. But by the end of October, they were called in for a conference with Rob's teacher.

"Rob is capable of doing the work," Ms. Wilson, the kindergarten teacher, said, "but he has trouble paying attention and staying on task. Instead, he spends a lot of time staring out the window or wandering around the room."

Mr. and Mrs. Eagen were concerned, too. In the short time since Rob had started school, their enthusiastic and well-adjusted child had turned into a tense and tired complainer.

"Rob is exhausted when he gets home," his mother told Ms. Wilson. "He picks on his younger brother, because he's jealous that his brother can stay home. He complains all the time about school. And he's having 'accidents' at night again—after staying dry for two years. Our pediatrician said the problem will go away once Rob gets used to school, but it hasn't. What can we do?"

"Rob is one of the very youngest children in the class," Ms. Wilson replied, "and I think he still needs to do a lot of his learning through play. The problem is that we have to do a lot more academic work in kindergarten than we used to, so the children will be ready to meet the state standards in first grade."

Ms. Wilson recommended that Rob's parents keep him in the kindergarten class with the understanding that some of the curriculum and instruction would be "differentiated" for Rob, so that he could work at a more comfortable level and learn in a more comfortable way. She added that children develop at different rates, and because Rob was an intelligent boy, he might suddenly "pick up the pace" during the year.

Rob's parents agreed, and at first their decision seemed to be the right one. At school, he completed some of his work and—more important to him—found a friend, someone he could swap food with at snack time and play with at recess. But when it came time for "hard work," Rob always began to fidget, wanting to sharpen pencils or go to the bathroom or talk to his friend. At home, Rob stopped picking on his brother, stopped wetting his bed, and started sharing stories about school. But he continued to exhibit signs of tension, reluctance, and anxiety about school.

In the spring, Ms. Wilson told his parents that Rob had made good progress in kindergarten but would need to make a big adjustment in order to succeed in first grade, where there was a greater amount of—and greater emphasis on—academic work. Mrs. Eagen was concerned about Rob's readiness for first grade, but Ms. Wilson said that socially it would be better for Rob to keep moving through the grades with his classmates, and he would probably catch up with them academically by third grade.

The Eagens decided to risk it. They knew their son was smart, and they wanted to believe he had made sufficient gains. Ms. Wilson encouraged them to do a lot of reading with Rob over the summer and also find him some appropriate workbooks that they could work on together, so he would be better prepared for the big change ahead.

Rob's "graduation" from kindergarten was cause for relief, if not rejoicing. He had made it! But Rob and his parents all remained quietly concerned about what would happen in first grade.

Excerpts from Robert Eagen's School Record—
Kindergarten

First term: Robert is one of the youngest children in the class. He accomplishes very little, though he's bright and very verbal. His immaturity is expressed in crying and an inability to stay on task.

Second term: Robert remains very unhappy in an academically oriented kindergarten program. His parents feel school-related stress is at the root of some behavioral problems at home.

Third term: Differentiating the program has had a positive effect on Robert. He's achieving more and feeling better about school.

Fourth term: Robert continues to improve, but he has not mastered all the concepts and skills needed for a strong start in first grade. I recommended that Robert's parents do some additional work with him over the summer to help him continue making progress.

Grade assignment: Rob is promoted to first grade.

Welcome to first grade

In September, Rob was assigned to an experienced teacher, Mrs. Fuller, a veteran of 22 years. Rob's dad had told the principal, "We want him with Mrs. Fuller. If anyone can get him up to speed, she can." Rob's anxiety level was high as he remembered what had happened at this time last year, but he went willingly off to school on the first day.

Mrs. Fuller knew that Rob needed monitoring, so she seated him near the front of the class. He liked sitting close to her desk, where he could see the pictures in the books she read to the class every day. What he disliked was sitting near two girls who were nearly a year older than he was, and who seemed a whole lot smarter. They actually loved school!

First grade became harder and harder for Rob. At home he burst into tears over the least little thing. One evening he confided to his mother that he wasn't as smart as the other children. His mother tenderly assured him that he was very smart—he just needed "to try a little harder" and soon he would catch up with the rest. Inwardly Rob's mother sighed. What had happened to this child, who had been so quick to learn and so filled with energy and confidence before he entered school?

Mrs. Fuller initiated a conference late in the fall. "Robert is certainly intelligent," she said, "but at this stage of his development it's going to be a real struggle for him to do the type of work required in first grade. A particular area of concern is that with the new standards, there is now an expectation that we see more progress with reading than Rob has demonstrated at this point in the year."

Rob's parents were not ready to accept what Mrs. Fuller told them. Surely, Mr. Eagen said, if they cooperated with the school, if they worked with Rob on reading at home, if they put him to bed earlier, if they took away his TV privileges and restricted his computer games, if they hired a tutor, if they were all tougher on him—surely then Rob could start to catch up and get back on track.

Mrs. Fuller had her doubts, but when his parents resisted her suggestion that they reconsider Rob's grade placement, she agreed to keep working intensively with Rob and recommended that he also start working with the school's reading specialist.

Once again, things were on the upswing—temporarily. Closely monitored and kept under constant pressure, Rob could accomplish average work. He liked receiving extra help, and with the reading specialist's assistance he began making more progress with reading. But he knew he still wasn't doing as well as expected. Sometimes the harder he tried, the more mistakes he made. That made him feel helpless and stupid. And sometimes he just didn't want to try at all.

In March, Mr. and Mrs. Eagen heard exactly what they did not want to hear. Mrs. Fuller wanted to retain Rob. His achievements and skills were significantly below grade level, and she was concerned that he would continue falling further behind, rather than suddenly catching up a few years later. She also thought his self-concept—already low—might suffer even more if he was promoted and had to spend another year trying to catch up.

Rob's parents were concerned about his self-concept, too. "If he's left back, he'll really feel like a failure," his mother said. "And he'll miss his friends terribly."

"Why not try him in second grade?" his father asked. "It's usually more of a catch-up year, anyhow. Then, if he doesn't reach the level he needs to be at for third grade, we might let him repeat second grade."

Mrs. Fuller pointed out that in order to prepare students for the mandated statewide tests in third grade, the second grade curriculum had become much more intensive and advanced than it was in the past. But Mr. Eagen felt he needed to protect his son from being "stigmatized" and "flunked" at such an early age.

Over Mrs. Fuller's reservations, Rob was promoted "on trial." His parents agreed to have him work with a tutor on finishing his first grade work over the summer, which made Rob feel cheated. Now he had to spend his vacation on all that stuff he hated most—math, phonics, and reading. At 6 years old, life wasn't fair.

Excerpts from Robert Eagen's School Record—
Grade One

First term: Robert has a good grasp of number and letter concepts but has difficulty concentrating. He seems developmentally young for first grade, showing little interest in pencil/paper tasks.

Second term: Robert's work habits are inconsistent—he does well one day, poorly the next two. I'm referring him for special help in reading three days a week, and he's seeing a tutor after school twice a week.

Third term: Still very young and sometimes very unhappy, Robert has a poor self-concept and is doing below-grade work. A good candidate for two years in first grade.

Fourth term: Robert has not made the progress needed to succeed in second grade. I've recommended that he take another year to complete first grade.

Grade assignment: Promoted to grade two on trial. Parents are obliged to see that he completes grade one work before September, with help from a tutor.

Welcome to second grade

Within two weeks after school opened, Mr. and Mrs. Eagen sensed that a storm was brewing. Their son complained, "Ms. Ruiz teaches too fast; she never explains things; she doesn't give me enough time."

Early in October they met with the teacher, whose concerns sounded like an indictment:

"Rob rarely completes his work...He doesn't follow instructions well...His verbal self-defense borders on backtalk...His attention span is very short...He once tore up a paper in frustration...He has behaved aggressively toward other children..."

Mr. and Mrs. Eagen were devastated. Maybe there was something wrong with the school, they thought, or with the teacher—maybe the teacher didn't like Rob. They requested a meeting with the principal, guidance counselor, and teacher, during which all agreed to have Rob evaluated.

To no one's surprise, an intelligence test showed that Rob's I.Q. was well above average, even though he was about six months behind academically. The assessment of his developmental level indicated that he was not yet ready for his current grade place- ment. The principal recommended that Rob take two years to complete second grade.

Rob's dad replied firmly, "After everything we've done to get him to this point, I can't see letting him flunk now. The tests show how intelligent he is, so letting him be held back doesn't seem like the right choice—except as a very last resort. Can't you people come up with an acceptable alternative?"

"There are some additional steps we can take," the principal said, "but with the current state standards and accountability testing, there are real limits to how much longer we can let this go on. Within the next two years, Rob is going to have to be performing at grade level and earning satisfactory scores on the state tests, or we will be required to retain him."

"Let's deal with that when we have to," Rob's father said, "and see what else we can do in the meantime."

Ms. Ruiz devised a differentiated instruction plan for Rob. Each week the boy signed a "contract" outlining tasks to be done, with rewards and consequences built in. He continued to be "pulled out" of class three times a week for sessions with the reading specialist. But now, in addition, he also met once a week with the guidance counselor, Mr. Hall.

To everyone's relief, the rigid academic structure, continued work with the reading specialist, and weekly meetings with Mr. Hall seemed to help Rob do better. With great effort, he finished enough of the second grade curriculum to be promoted, as long as he fulfilled a mandatory obligation to attend summer school. Sadly, he faced two more months of math, phonics, and reading, while many of his classmates looked forward to a real summer vacation. His schedule allowed little time off for play.

Excerpts from Robert Eagen's School Record—
Grade Two

First term: Robert is often over his head, unable to follow directions or finish work. His behavior reveals significant frustration.

Second term: Robert was referred for further testing. Results indicate that he's developmentally young, despite superior intelligence. Rob is under contract to carry out a differentiated instructional plan in math and language arts. He'll continue to receive special reading help and after-school tutoring. Mr. Hall will shore up his confidence.

Third term: The plan put in place for Rob is enabling him to make progress, but he continues to lag behind many of his classmates, and this sometimes results in his having problems with them.

Fourth term: Rob functions well in class only when under pressure and receiving substantial support. His performance and skills remain far below grade level.

Grade assignment: Promoted to third grade on trial. Summer school mandatory.

Welcome to third grade

On the opening day of classes, it was Mrs. Eagen's turn to cry as she watched Rob go off to school. He had just promised her, "I'm really going to try hard this year. I won't be bad anymore." Forcing Rob to go to school like this just isn't right, Mrs. Eagen thought. My boy is really hurting.

Minutes after Rob reached school that morning, he listened to Mrs. Resnick outline her plans for the year, and he knew he was in deep trouble.

"As third graders, you will learn to tell time to the minute without digital watches," she said. "You will learn to use cursive lettering without mixing in manuscript letters...you will do four book reports independently, in addition to your other homework...you will be required to use correct spelling rather than inventive spelling on your reports, and there will be weekly spelling lists and tests to help you make progress...you will learn your multiplication tables for 0–12, and also start working on division and fractions. We'll also be doing some special units to make sure everyone does well on the statewide language arts and math tests during the winter and spring."

When Rob came home that day, his mother took one look at him and knew the whole story. He ran to her in tears. "I'll never be able to do all the stupid third grade work! Third grade is dumb." Mrs. Eagen held Rob close. We're always pushing him and pushing him, she thought, and it's just too hard for him. I know we're making a serious mistake.

That evening Rob's mother shared her concerns with her husband, but he still saw changing their position as giving up on their son and conceding defeat. "Look," he said, "set up an appointment with Mrs. Resnick, and we'll see what she has to say about Rob."

When they met with Mrs. Resnick, she was thoroughly familiar with Rob's school history—his situation was well documented.

"Third grade isn't just a year in which the children are expected to learn a lot of new things," she explained. "It's also the grade in which the children are expected to finish up much of what they've been working on throughout the primary grades. There's an old saying that from kindergarten through third grade, the emphasis is on learning to read, but from fourth grade on, the emphasis is on reading to learn. With our state standards, that's truer than ever. I'm concerned that Rob isn't far enough along yet to handle all the new material this year and do well on the state tests. That also makes it likely that he won't be ready for the other big changes that will be happening next year."

"But with all the support Rob's been getting and all the hard work he's done, we can't just give up now," Rob's father said. "Besides, isn't this the year when kids like him are supposed to catch up with everyone else?"

Mrs. Resnick smiled sadly. "I know some people used to say that all the kids would catch up in third grade, but I've never heard a third grade teacher say that, and I've never seen it happen in my class or anyone else's. There's always a range of chronological ages and developmental stages in every grade, and while some children do seem to accelerate at certain points, the differences don't just disappear. In Rob's case, he's far enough below grade level that meeting the third grade standards by the end of the year would be a tremendous accomplishment, and there are some other students in the class who will be ready to start doing fourth grade work soon. But the important thing as far as Rob's concerned is that we're no longer allowed to keep promoting students who don't meet the standards and pass the state tests."

"Well," Mr. Eagen said, "why don't we at least give him a try, and if he isn't doing grade-level work by the end of year, it sounds like we may not have any choice in the matter, anyhow."

Mrs. Resnick was willing to do some additional work with Rob, who would also continue receiving support from the reading specialist, the guidance counselor, and an after-school tutor. Reluctantly, Rob's mother agreed with the decision to keep Rob where he was.

Despite everyone's best efforts, Rob fell further behind. Because he had never truly completed the second grade curriculum, he did not have the solid foundation needed to master the new concepts and skills required for success in third grade. His frustration continued to increase, while his attitude, behavior, and grades deteriorated even further.

For his parents, life seemed to drag along from one school conference to the next. They wondered if they had failed their son. They wondered how long they could endure the nightly tussles with homework, as well as Rob's complaints, bad behavior, and obvious unhappiness.

In December, Rob's parents were invited to an evening meeting, sponsored by the PTA, on the subject of school success and school failure. There they heard a speaker outline the concepts of developmental readiness and proper grade placement, and they listened as parents whose children had taken an additional year to learn and grow endorsed this approach enthusiastically.

After the meeting, Mrs. Eagen said firmly, "I know that Rob needs an additional year before fourth grade."

"Those other kids probably aren't as smart as Rob," Mr. Eagen said. "He's working really hard right now, and I think if we all hang in there, he'll make it." But deep down inside, Mr. Eagen was beginning to suspect that his wife was right and that it was time to stop forcing Rob to struggle so much.

For Rob, recess was the only thing that made school endurable. The second and third grades had recess together, and Rob enjoyed spending time with some of the second graders more than with his classmates. He began to feel like the second graders were his real friends, and one spring morning he asked if he could spend the day with his "old" second grade teacher, Mrs. Ruiz. After first checking with her, Mrs. Resnick granted his request.

After school that day, Rob talked nonstop about the great time he'd had in school and how easy it was. For once he felt like one of the smartest kids in the class. For once he could finish his assignments.

At the supper table Rob's father was stunned as he listened to his son's enthusiasm for school bubbling over. "Can I go back to Mrs. Ruiz's class again next week?" Rob asked.

There was silence at the table as Mr. Eagen considered his son's request. Rob's happiness was so evident that Mr. Eagen's resistance suddenly and finally crumbled. "Rob, let me ask you something," Mr. Eagen said very seriously. "Would you like to keep visiting Mrs. Ruiz's class this spring, and then be with that class in third grade all next year?"

Would he! The idea of being smart, successful, and in class with his friends made his spirits soar, but then the boy hesitated and said softly, "Some of the other kids are going to make fun of me if I stay back a year. They think I'm stupid anyway."

Mr. Eagen promised that he and Rob's mother would help Rob learn how to talk about the change, and that they would have the school principal, teachers, and guidance counselor speak to the other children.

With the same determination that he had insisted on Rob's staying in third grade, Mr. Eagen now supported the decision to repeat third grade. He knew it was right for Rob, and he could see how it would enable Rob to achieve the success in school they had all wanted for so long. And Rob knew—from his father's tone and his mother's smile—that he had the support of the people who were most important in his world.

Over the next few weeks, it was surprisingly easy to arrange to make the changes they had discussed. Mrs. Ruiz was happy to have Rob visiting her class and mastering the skills he had struggled with last year. Mrs. Resnick explained to her third grade class that what Rob was doing was similar to visiting one of the specialists that many of them spent time with every week. And late in the spring, she, Ms. Ruiz, and Mr. Hall spoke with the second and third graders, saying it was perfectly all right for a boy or girl to spend an additional year in a grade. Because a number of students did it almost every year, the other children were used to it, and that made the situation somewhat easier for Rob.

Rob did have to deal with some teasing from other children, but because his parents had prepared him and because he was so relieved to be out of the hopeless situation he had been in before, it didn't bother him as much as he expected. When Lance, a third grader, purposely bumped into him on the playground and said,

"Get out of my way, dummy," Rob just thought to himself, *I'm not going to let it bother me too much. I know it wasn't my fault that I couldn't do all the work. Next year I'll start showing everyone how smart I really am.*

Rob's mother had explained to him that his problems in school were not his fault—and never had been his fault. She blamed herself and his father for making him try to do work he wasn't ready for. Their intentions were good and they had done what they thought was right—after all, don't most parents start their children in school when the school officials tell them to? Someone had to be the youngest in the class. But they had made a mistake by insisting that he keep moving up a grade each year, even when he hadn't really completed the work and was so unhappy. Now they were asking him to help correct the mistake. And they wanted to make sure he knew that they loved him very much.

Excerpts from Robert Eagen's School Record— Grade Three

First term: Rob has a negative attitude and seems totally overwhelmed. He lacks the academic skills and level of maturity needed to meet the third grade standards.

Second term: Rob's parents are supportive and work with him every night, but Rob is still far below grade level and falling further behind.

Third term: Rob's academic work and attitude are both poor. He is very unlikely to complete the third grade curriculum and be ready for fourth grade this year.

Fourth term: Rob's attitude has greatly improved, and he is also accomplishing more, now that he is spending time brushing up on second grade work.

Grade assignment: Rob is taking an additional year to complete third grade.

Welcome to third grade (one more time)

As the first day of school approached, Rob felt some of the familiar dread he had come to associate with starting a new school year, but overall he felt much better than he had in years past. For one thing, he had enjoyed a real summer vacation this year, spending his days with friends at camp and with his family on a trip to the ocean, rather than with other unhappy students in summer school—or with a tutor and an endless series of flash cards.

But even more important, he felt good about being back in the same classroom with Mrs. Resnick and his friends from second grade, where he knew the routines and thought he might just be able to do all the work this year. And he was sure it would be better than moving on to a new teacher and classroom with different routines and even harder assignments, which he knew deep down inside he just wouldn't be able to do well. Sure, there might be some more teasing or meanness because he was repeating a grade, but there had already been teasing and meanness when he couldn't do his work in the previous grades. Now at least he had a chance of doing well.

Mrs. Resnick helped get the year off to a good start by making Rob her special assistant, who helped the other students learn the routines at the start of the year. For once he was the one who knew more than the others, and as the academic work began to intensify, he found that he could keep up with the others. He began to think to himself with amazement and delight, *I can do this*, and sometimes he even thought, *I'm one of the best in the class at this*.

Some things take more time to work out, however. Children who are over their heads in school develop poor work habits that are reinforced as they move up through the grades. Rob, for example, had developed the habit of frequently asking for directions to be repeated. This habit originated from his restlessness, which made it hard for him to listen, and on some occasions from a true lack of understanding. Also, asking a question often worked as a stalling tactic, keeping him from having to deal immediately with his work. Habits are hard to break, and it took a lot of effort before Rob was able—nearly always—to listen well and then get right to work the first time around.

In addition, during his first attempt at third grade, he had developed a need to disappear into the bathroom soon after the teacher announced math work. Little by little, over time, Rob was able to overcome this habit, too. His self-confidence was on the upswing, and after the first few weeks of school everyone agreed that he no longer needed to have weekly sessions with the guidance counselor.

His behavior and moods improved at home, too. He had time to play after school because his parents had decided to hold off on after-school tutoring until they could see if it was needed. And his parents no longer had to keep after him to complete his homework. He was more willing to sit down and do it—and usually he actually could do it. Everyone felt a huge sense of relief, especially when the first tests and reports Rob brought home had much better grades and comments than ever before.

The first parent conference with Mrs. Resnick was also a relief. Instead of the usual litany of bad news, they all talked about the improvements they were seeing. And when they talked about areas that needed further improvement, there was a growing confidence that the further improvements actually could and would occur—without extreme measures and extensive support. There was also a particularly welcome moment for Rob's parents when Mrs. Resnick mentioned that much of Rob's work was now close to grade level, and she was hopeful that he would be at or even slightly above grade level by the end of the year.

As the year continued, Rob no longer dreaded bringing home his report cards, and the Eagens' refrigerator became so plastered with Rob's schoolwork that it looked like the supermarket bulletin board. Late in the winter, they happily cleared a space on the fridge and added the certificate documenting Rob's "graduation" from the reading group. He no longer had to be pulled out of class or see any tutors after school, because he could do grade level work on his own.

During the first week of the statewide tests, Rob's stomach had acted up a little in the morning, but his confidence increased as the week progressed and he began to feel that he was answering a lot of the questions correctly. He felt even better about the second week of tests, and he felt best of all when Mrs. Resnick reviewed the results with him and said they showed that he was ready for fourth grade.

Excerpts from Robert Eagen's School Record—
Grade Three

First term: Rob is more focused and much happier than he was at this time last year. The quality of his work is improving, and so are his social interactions.

Second term: Rob is completing all of his assignments satisfactorily and shows few signs of the problems he experienced in the past. His parents report that he's "like a new child" at home.

Third term: Rob is now doing grade-level work in almost all areas. His work shows care, and he is now mastering concepts and skills that were previously too challenging for him.

Fourth term: Rob's best term ever. He is now in the top half of his class academically and is demonstrating initiative in his work with his fellow students. He also did well on the statewide language arts and math tests.

Grade assignment: Rob is promoted to fourth grade unconditionally.

Living "happily ever after..." (with a few exceptions)

By the time he neared the end of his elementary school experience, Rob's poor work habits and signs of stress had all but vanished. He was one of the top students in his class, his teachers were pleased with his attitude as well as his performance, and he had good friends in his grade.

A trace of his early experience lingered on in his answer when someone innocently asked him which grade he was in. Like many other children who have taken more than one year to complete a grade, Rob invariably replied, "I'm in the fifth grade, but I'm supposed to be in sixth." This is the apology of a child who has felt like a failure—a child who needs to hear, "You are right where you are supposed to be."

Mr. and Mrs. Eagen have not yet fully recovered from the trauma of their boy's start in school, and possibly they never will. His mother occasionally looks at Rob and wonders to herself, "Why didn't I listen to him and my own concerns when Rob so clearly communicated how he felt during his first years in school? When he still couldn't do the work even though we knew he was intelligent and trying hard, how could we have kept acting like there was something wrong with him and not the situation he was in? Of course, now the idea of wrong grade placement makes so much sense, because he's clearly in the right grade and doing above-grade-level work. But back then it was hard to understand, and standing up against the system was hard, too. Still, it was our child who was suffering, and we should have seen what was happening and done something sooner."

Rob's father sometimes thinks, "Was it my stiff-necked pride that made me insist for so long on Rob's not taking extra time? Was it my fear of what my father and other people would think about my son? Or was it my real concern for the boy? I remember when I was in school—how fearful I was of being left back, how relieved I was to be promoted when those report cards were issued at the end of the year, and how mean we were to the kids who didn't make it. Now I understand how unimportant all of that is. Who cares what some people think about Rob's grade placement, as long as he's happy and successful? From now on, my boy's true needs come first."

By the time Rob's younger brother—who was born in July—was old enough to enter kindergarten, the school had several options available that offered a supportive, additional year of learning time. And having learned from their first son's experiences, the Eagens responded positively and without hesitation to the recommendation that their younger son take advantage of the opportunity to experience school success right from the start.

Rewriting the past— and changing the future

Had Rob been placed properly in school right at the beginning— based on his developmental needs and capabilities, rather than just his chronological age—his introduction to school would have been a much more positive experience, and each succeeding year another building block of success. Being placed in the wrong grade not only had a very negative impact on Rob's academic career and family life, it also deeply affected his sense of himself and his feelings about other students.

Obviously, children's initial placement in school is far too important to be determined just by the number of candles on their birthday cakes. But relying solely on a child's age at some arbitrary school entrance cut-off date is still the system used by many schools to make initial grade placement decisions. And while other schools use a much more fair and accurate approach, individual educators and parents always have the right—and responsibility—to consider grade placement decisions thoroughly and explore alternatives, no matter what system is in place.

The following chapter provides guidelines and questionnaires that can help educators and parents evaluate the full range of information needed to make these crucial decisions for the children in their care.

CHAPTER 4

What Wrong Grade Placement Looks Like: Signs and Signals of an Overplaced Student

With their facial expressions, their bodies, and their behavior—not just their words—students communicate their needs. For example, any parent knows what it means when a young child's bottom lip begins to quiver. And most teachers and parents recognize a variety of ways students indicate they are feeling happy or sad, energetic or exhausted, full of mischief or miserable. Children constantly make statements about themselves through their behavior.

Even when children try to conceal their feelings, they usually are not very good at it. Without meaning to, they "give away" their inner state through their body language, letting parents and teachers pick up the cues. These silent signals are often calls for help, but sometimes society's expectations may blind us to the messages a child is transmitting.

This chapter can help you train yourself to recognize the signs and signals of students placed in the wrong grade or program at school. Remember that recognizing the distress of such students is the first step toward extricating them from a bad situation—and enabling them to succeed.

One size doesn't always fit all

Students in any grade come in a great variety of shapes and sizes—tall, short, plump, lean, large, medium, small. Can you imagine the principal of a school ignoring all of these physical differences and insisting that all the students in a grade wear the same size shoes?

The way you fit into your shoes and the way you fit into a grade both affect your growth and comfort when you are young. Shoes that don't fit can cause considerable damage, hurting children physically, contributing to emotional and social discomfort, and distracting children intellectually. In addition, ill-fitting shoes might just affect the way a child walks through the rest of his or her life. In contrast, proper-fitting shoes give their wearer a firm and secure basis for proceeding, just as the proper fit in a grade or program gives a student a solid educational foundation.

Of course, no school principal would consider forcing all the students in a grade to wear the same size shoes. But administrators routinely adopt a "one-size-fits-all" approach to grade placement, leaving some mismatched students with permanent problems.

One rationale for taking this approach is that a teacher can "individualize" or "differentiate" the curriculum and instruction. Unfortunately, class sizes remain high in many schools, and even if the class size is smaller, the diversity of America's students—their differing interests, talents, academic achievements, developmental stages, and cultural backgrounds—is being further complicated by the "full inclusion" of severely handicapped children, who previously would have been in small special education classes taught by teachers prepared specifically to work with such children. Meanwhile, strict adherence to a mandated curriculum is now required by many school districts, as is intensive test prep prior to standardized tests.

Under these circumstances, a teacher would have to be quite a miracle worker to provide individualized instruction to such a wide range of children and have them all meet the same state standards in the exact same amount of time. While most teachers actually accomplish an amazing amount during the school year, there are some things even they cannot do. For no matter how much a teacher pushes or individualizes, no matter how much pressure the parents exert, no matter how malleable the students, all children simply cannot be forced to develop and learn at the same rate. And the reality is that kids "get all bent out of shape" when they are put under intense pressure to succeed at the same time their developmental and educational needs are *not* being met.

Train yourself to detect wrong grade placement

Children who wear the wrong size shoes compensate by walking in distorted ways. Similarly, students in the wrong grade or program respond in ways that will help them survive the experience—but that interfere with their capacity to succeed in school and lead happy, productive lives. While their lives are being distorted in this way, their bodies and/or emotions often exhibit signs that the students are experiencing too much school-related stress and therefore need adult intervention.

Once you train yourself to detect signs of wrong grade placement, you still may not be sure how seriously to take them. But if you notice that the student *consistently* exhibits *numerous* signs of school-related stress over an *extended* period of time—such as an ongoing combination of frustration, anxiety, and extensive academic difficulties—then you have a responsibility to explore the possibility that the student is in the wrong grade. In many cases, this exploration will confirm what you have suspected in your heart all along: the student is in deep water and may be sinking fast, so a rescue effort needs to start *now*.

Remember, though, that all students display some signs of stress from time to time. The real clues to serious trouble are consistency and multiplicity. And remember, too, that students who have an attention deficit disorder or learning disability—or who are clinically depressed—may exhibit signs similar to those of students who are in the wrong grade or program. In fact, some students who have been identified as "educationally handicapped" turn out to be "educationally superior" when provided with an appropriate grade placement and an opportunity to develop at their own rate. And some students who seem to have an attention deficit disorder may really be having trouble concentrating because they are not yet capable of comprehending the curriculum and/or coping with the methods of instruction currently being used. There may also be overlapping or even conflicting signs that reflect a multiplicity of problems.

That's why it is important to take a thorough look at student behavior, rather than just considering one limited viewpoint, and why the signs of wrong grade placement described in the next few pages are organized in three different ways:
- developmental signs—physical, emotional, social, intellectual/academic
- "covert" signs
- signs by age level

These different perspectives are not meant to be mutually exclusive. Instead, they should be used together to obtain a full understanding of the "whole child." Start by reading through the next few pages, keeping in mind that a student who consistently exhibits these signs is likely to be having trouble at home as well as in school, which compounds the amount of stress he or she is experiencing.

Listen carefully to such a student and watch for behavior patterns. As you do, trust your innate common sense and good judgment. Let your understanding of the child guide you in making the tough decisions that are likely to shape his or her life.

Developmental signs of wrong grade placement

Children's physical, emotional, social and intellectual/academic growth are four key aspects of their overall development. Students who need more time to develop and learn before succeeding in a particular grade or program may exhibit their unhappiness through any or all of these aspects. The signs and signals in this section have been compiled into "portraits" that may help you identify particular students in need of help. The portraits will also help you understand how overplaced students latch on to certain stratagems in order to survive the misery of being mismatched with a grade or program.

Students exhibiting physical signs of wrong grade placement

Frowning, squinting, a clenched jaw...this sort of facial expression reflects a student's misery in school. He or she may also appear to be burdened by "the weight of the world" on hunched shoulders.

A student of this sort often hears everything going on inside (and outside) the classroom—except the teacher's instructions. The student may hear only the last half of the instructions or may insist, "The teacher never told us to do that." He or she frequently needs to have directions repeated again and again—and again.

Always on the go, this student uses constant physical movement to release tension. He or she is easily distracted and loves "in-house field trips" to the pencil sharpener and other relaxing destinations. If allowed, this student would make ten trips a day to

61

visit and/or help the school custodian. (Adults may suspect the student of having an attention deficit disorder with hyperactivity, when in fact he or she may simply be feeling the effects of wrong grade placement and trying to "work out" some of the related stress.)

For younger students who are overplaced, school is frequently a physical struggle. Their writing is laborious; they quickly grow tired; they cannot sit through a twenty-minute reading lesson, much less a six-hour day. Often they will try to negotiate: "Hey, teacher, can I write just a little bit and not the whole sentence?"

Some of these students learn to hate writing—with good reason. Their fine-motor skills are not yet fully developed, so they take too long to complete written assignments, they make holes in the paper from constant erasing, and they mix cursive and manuscript writing, as well as capital and lower-case letters. For these students, writing is so difficult it literally hurts.

Reading also tends to be difficult for these students, so they try to avoid both reading and writing whenever they can. When they must read and/or write, they may invert, reverse, omit, and substitute letters and words.

Daily demands that cannot be met take their toll on a student's energy. Some students may miss school frequently because of exhaustion. Younger students may fall asleep during afternoon story time or need after-school naps.

Wrong grade placement may also result in low resistance to illness. First graders in particular seem predisposed to morning stomachaches and colds. Feeling excessive pressure to do the impossible might further depress an already overtaxed autoimmune system.

Students exhibiting emotional signs of wrong grade placement

These students constantly seek adult approval and reassurance. Too filled with self-doubt to work independently, they want and need lots of praise for each little effort they make.

The student who always has to know "right now" if he's "right," even when it means interrupting the teacher, has a tremendous fear of making a mistake. This extreme concern about being wrong prevents the student from taking risks—even from volunteering answers. Living like a second-class citizen, he or she often does not have the confidence to try new endeavors.

Overplaced students are easily distracted and often lose their place in a lesson, or give the right answer to the wrong question—their bodies are there, but their minds have "gone fishing." Put another way, recurrent daydreaming becomes an escape mechanism that helps emotionally stressed students get through another day in the wrong grade.

These students often lack confidence in their physical ability to measure up to other students. Fearful of getting hurt, overplaced students may avoid contact sports. If the fear is strong enough, a younger student may complain when accidentally touched by another student. Sometimes picked on by classmates, these students feel inferior and suffer from low self-esteem.

A student experiencing emotional stress also cries easily, because crying helps to release tension. When school work seems too hard, or when the student is scolded or otherwise feels threatened, tears may quickly appear, revealing how developmentally young he or she truly is. Transitions and social situations can be especially difficult for this student to handle.

Nailbiting may also occur, as having a hand in the mouth aids a nervous child in "handling" anxiety. Other signs of nervousness include frequent throat clearing, coughing, eye blinking, and bed-wetting. Among older students, particularly preadolescent and adolescent girls, a more recent phenomenon is skin cutting.

Some students in the wrong grade may actually behave very well at school but then act out at home, although their behavior at home improves during school holidays and vacations. The difference in home and school behavior is so extreme, parents may think they are hearing a case of mistaken identity when the teacher describes their own child. In reality, the student's emotional repression at school is resulting in extensive emotional release at home.

Students exhibiting social signs of wrong grade placement

These students stay on the sidelines, avoiding other students in the same grade. They do not seem to fit in with their peer group and often feel unaccepted and rejected.

A student who feels "pushed aside" in this way may push back at others in retaliation, or "act up" in ways that are annoying. Hurt and left out, this student may sometimes lash out in anger and jealousy at successful classmates. He or she may become a bully, obtaining attention—even though it's negative—and demonstrating a superiority over the other kids in at least one respect.

These students actually feel smaller and weaker than others their age. This is due in part to weaker academic performance, but also to weak social skills. Having few friends and not knowing what others expect, he or she feels uncomfortable in social situations. He may seek out younger children because his interests are like theirs, and he is likely to enjoy visiting a grade lower than his own. She would rather play alone than take chances competing.

Passive and apathetic, this sort of student usually takes no initiative in class, drifting along with what others do. At home, the child's favorite activity is watching television.

Students exhibiting intellectual/academic signs of wrong grade placement

Constantly playing "catch up," overplaced students cannot complete their work in a reasonable amount of time. And when new concepts or skills are introduced, these students have inordinate trouble understanding and integrating them. Students in this situation may also continue to appear "lost" long after classmates have demonstrated mastery and moved on.

One result of their incomprehension is that overplaced students have difficulty staying on task. Instead of "getting into the flow" intellectually, they quickly become exhausted from all their struggling and anxiety. Then they are the first to let the rest of the class know when it's time for recess or lunch.

Some students do very well one day but poorly the next. Brains are not their problem—in many cases they are bright but too young developmentally to keep up the pace and continue moving ahead to higher levels of learning and performance.

In order to survive in school, these students use their intellectual powers to invent reasons for not meeting expectations:
"The teacher said it wasn't due today."
"I did the work last night but forgot to bring it to school."
"Someone must have taken my homework."

Parents may blame the teacher for "not challenging" the student, who claims that school is "too easy" or "boring." The truth, however, is that the pressure is too much for the student. It might even lead to a "lost" or altered report card.

"She has the potential but won't apply herself." "He could do the work, but he's just plain lazy." When parents or teachers find themselves saying things like this at a school conference, it's an indication that the real problem may be a lack of readiness.

And if one or more of the following descriptions also applies to the student, there is even more reason to consider the possibility of wrong grade placement:

- significantly below grade level in multiple subject areas
- frequently has difficulty processing information and transferring learning to other subject areas
- often unable to grasp new or abstract concepts.

Students who don't make waves may still need rescuing

Of course, not all overplaced students behave alike, but all such students do exhibit signs that something is wrong. The way in which a particular student reveals these signs and signals depends upon his or her individual personality, as well as on family upbringing and the classroom environment. Some students who feel oppressed by school react *overtly*, clearly showing how and what they feel. Other students become withdrawn and express their distress in a *covert* manner. In either case, what the student is experiencing is very painful and very real, and in many cases it is not a problem that the student alone can solve.

Some students who appear to be passive or "too good to be true" may actually feel too frightened and vulnerable to reveal themselves. The resulting covert stress signs present a particular challenge to adults, because these signs are difficult to detect, let alone interpret.

Remember that certain types of children under stress are more likely to show their unhappiness in covert ways. These include:

- children who are bright intellectually but immature in their social, emotional, or physical development
- girls who have been raised in the "good little girl" tradition
- children who have been experiencing undue pressure to perform and succeed
- "hurried" children who take on adult roles.

In addition, concerned adults should keep a watchful eye on the following types of students, whose behavior—if accompanied by significantly below-grade performance in a number of subject areas—may be an indication of wrong grade placement:

- a student who is apathetic, passive, unresponsive, or ultra-obedient
- a student who seems bored, unmotivated, or just "goes through the motions"
- a student who does little but read or who focuses exclusively on academic study
- a student who seldom participates in class or other activities, striving to go unnoticed
- a student who talks "a blue streak" but avoids writing
- a student who avoids challenge and competition
- a student who often postpones work.

Age-level signs and signals of wrong grade placement

Children who are in the wrong grade or program typically display certain signs and signals at each age level. Some of the signs are unique to particular ages; other signs—such as "develops a nervous tic"—span several ages.

As you review the following checklists, you may "recognize" one or more children who have reached the age indicated and display signs or signals for that age. A child who displays only a few of these behavior patterns may be under considerable stress. Do remember, though, that all children occasionally fit some of the descriptions. It is only when a child *consistently* displays *several* signs of stress for an *extended* period of time that adults need to be concerned.

Many educators have found these checklists to be a helpful framework for observing children and discussing individual children with their parents. For these purposes, the checklists for each age level are in a format suitable for individual use. In particular, space is provided to note whether the specific behaviors *never* occur, *rarely* occur, or *often* occur. Analyzing the frequency of behaviors in this way can help to determine the overall severity of a child's school stress.

4-Year-Olds: Signs and signals of inappropriate placement

NEVER
RARELY
OFTEN

At Home
A 4-year-old in the wrong program at preschool may:

1. not want to leave Mom/Dad;

2. hide shoes so as not to have to go to preschool;

3. complain about stomachaches or headaches;

4. have bathroom "accidents";

5. come home exhausted;

6. have nightmares.

At Preschool
A 4-year-old in the wrong program may:

1. have difficulty separating from Mom/Dad;

2. cling to the teacher, showing a high degree of dependency;

3. not participate in "cooperative" play—instead, his or her play is "isolated" (child plays alone) or "parallel" (playing next to other children but not with them);

4. not like the other children;

5. show "young" fine-motor coordination while cutting, gluing, drawing, etc.;

6. demonstrate a lack of awareness of appropriate behavior in the "classroom";

7. not catch on to "classroom" routines, which more mature classmates adapt to easily;

8. find it difficult to select activities and stick with them;

9. become "outspoken" and/or want to leave when asked to perform a task that is too difficult.

In General
A 4-year-old in the wrong program may:

1. cry easily;

2. lack self-control or self-discipline (biting, hitting and kicking);

3. appear to be "shy";

4. revert to thumbsucking, nailbiting, or "baby talk";

5. become aggressive during games and other activities involving the taking of turns or sharing.

Evaluation: All children display some of these signs and signals at times. The possibility that a child is in the wrong program should be considered when the child consistently displays several signs or signals over an extended period of time. An example would be 3 or more signs or signals, occurring often for 2 or more weeks and increasingly interfering with the child's home, school, and social life.

5-Year-Olds: Signs and signals of wrong grade placement

At Home
A 5-year-old in the wrong grade or program may:

1.not want to leave Mom/Dad;
2. not want to go to school;
3. suffer from stomachaches or headaches, particularly in the morning before school;
4. dislike school or complain that school is "dumb";
5. claim that the teacher does not allow enough time to finish his or her school work;
6. need to rest, but resist taking a nap;
7. revert to bedwetting;
8. complain about having to stay in kindergarten for a full day.

At School
A 5-year-old in the wrong grade or program may:

1. show little interest in kindergarten "academics";
2. frequently ask if it's time to go home;
3. be unable to hold scissors as directed by the teacher;
4. worry that Mom will forget to pick him or her up after school;
5. have a difficult time following the daily routine;
6. talk incessantly;
7. complain that school work is "too hard" ("I can't do it,") or "too easy" ("It's so easy, I'm not going to do it,") or "too boring";
8. interrupt the teacher constantly;
9. be unable to shift easily from one task to the next;
10. be overly restless during class, and frequently in motion when supposed to be working at a task.

NEVER	RARELY	OFTEN	
			In General **A 5-year-old in the wrong grade or program may:**
			1. become withdrawn;
			2. revert to thumbsucking or infantile speech;
			3. compare herself negatively to other children ("They can do it, but I can't.");
			4. complain that he has no friends;
			5. cry easily and frequently;
			6. make up stories;
			7. bite his or her nails;
			8. seem depressed;
			9. tire easily.

Evaluation: All children display some of these signs and signals at times. The possibility that a child is in the wrong grade or program should be considered when the child consistently displays several signs or signals over an extended period of time. An example would be 3 or more signs or signals, occurring often for 2 or more weeks and increasingly interfering with the child's home, school, and social life.

6-Year-Olds: Signs and signals of wrong grade placement

At Home
A 6-year-old in the wrong grade may:

1. frequently complain of before-school stomachaches;

2. revert to bed-wetting;

3. behave in a manner that seems out of character to the parent or teacher;

4. frequently ask to stay at home.

At School
A 6-year-old in the wrong grade may:

1. prefer to play with younger children;

2. want to play with toys during class time;

3. choose recess, gym, and music as favorite subjects;

4. feel overwhelmed by the size and activity level of the lunchroom;

5. have a high rate of absenteeism;

6. try to take frequent "in-house field trips" to the pencil sharpener, bathroom, school nurse, custodian, etc.;

7. mark papers randomly;

8. "act out" on the playground;

9. reverse, invert, substitute, or omit letters and numbers when reading and/or writing (this is also not unusual for properly placed students, either);

10. complain about being bored with school work, when in reality he or she cannot do the work;

11. have a short attention span—be unable to stay focused on a twenty-minute lesson;

12. have difficulty understanding the teacher's instructions;

13. demonstrate extensive inability and resistance in regard to reading and arithmetic;

14. do work that is significantly below grade level in a number of subject areas.

NEVER	RARELY	OFTEN	
			In General **A 6-year-old in the wrong grade may:**
			1. cry easily and frequently;
			2. tire quickly;
			3. need constant reassurance and praise;
			4. become withdrawn and shy;
			5. develop a nervous tic—a twitching eye, a nervous cough, frequent clearing of the throat or twirling of hair;
			6. revert to thumbsucking;
			7. lie or "adjust the truth" about school;
			8. revert to soiling his or her pants;
			9. make restless body movements, such as rocking back and forth in a chair, jiggling legs, etc.;
			10. dawdle;
			11. seem depressed;
			12. feel harried/hurried.

Evaluation: All children display some of these signs and signals at times. The possibility that a student is in the wrong grade should be considered when the student consistently displays several signs or signals over an extended period of time. An example would be 3 or more signs or signals, occurring often for 2 or more weeks and increasingly interfering with the child's home, school, and social life.

7-Year-Olds: Signs and signals of wrong grade placement

NEVER
RARELY
OFTEN

At Home
A 7-year-old in the wrong grade may:

1. develop a psychosomatic illness, such as a stomachache, a headache, a sore leg, a limp, a "temp," etc.;

2. wet the bed or soil his/her pants;

3. develop a well-founded fear of going on to third grade;

4. frequently ask to stay at home.

At School
A 7-year-old in the wrong grade may:

1. prefer playing with younger children;

2. constantly erase his or her work (many 7-year-olds do a great deal of erasing);

3. try to create diversions from the work at hand;

4. frequently be absent;

5. act aggressively on the playground;

6. develop poor work habits, such as ripping up papers, losing papers, keeping a messy desk;

7. have difficulty staying with a task or lesson;

8. revert, invert, substitute, or omit letters and numbers when reading and/or writing;

9. feel badgered about reading;

10. be "consistently inconsistent" about work;

11. focus exclusively on one subject, such as math, and have no interest in other subjects;

12. do work that is significantly below grade level in a number of subject areas.

In General
A 7-year-old in the wrong grade may:

1. cry easily;

2. "stretch" the truth;

3. withdraw;

4. develop a nervous tic—a twitching eye, a nervous cough, frequent clearing of the throat or twirling of hair, etc.;

5. pull out his or her hair;

6. seem depressed;

7. complain about "everything."

Evaluation: All children display some of these signs and signals at times. The possibility that a student is in the wrong grade should be considered when the student consistently displays several signs or signals over an extended period of time. An example would be 3 or more signs or signals, occurring often for 2 or more weeks and increasingly interfering with the child's home, school, and social life.

NEVER
RARELY
OFTEN

8-Year-Olds: Signs and signals of wrong grade placement

At Home
An 8-year-old in the wrong grade may:

1. complain about "too much" school work;

2. pick on siblings;

3. develop a psychosomatic illness, such as a stomachache, a headache, a sore leg, a limp, a "temp," etc.;

4. be difficult to direct;

5. express concern about or try to avoid tests.

At School
An 8-year-old in the wrong grade may:

1. prefer to play with younger children;

2. dislike certain subjects (knowing that he or she is behind and doesn't know how to do the work);

3. write laboriously and find cursive writing extremely difficult;

4. feel overwhelmed by the volume of work;

5. seem incapable of working independently;

6. ask for permission to visit previous grade;

7. frequently say, "My old teacher did it this way";

8. find that even a reasonable amount of copying from the chalkboard is extremely difficult;

9. be unable to memorize the multiplication tables;

10. habitually lose or destroy papers;

11. find shifting to hardcover textbooks extremely difficult;

12. have difficulty with test-prep activities and exhibit signs of test-related anxiety;

13. do work that is significantly below grade level in a number of subject areas.

NEVER	RARELY	OFTEN	
			In General **An 8-year-old in the wrong grade may:**
			1. cherish toys and make them more important than is appropriate for his or her age;
			2. develop a nervous tic—a twitching eye, a nervous cough, frequent clearing of the throat or twirling of hair;
			3. not seem to fit into his or her peer group;
			4. take out frustrations on other children during play;
			5. be picked on or rejected by peers, and called names such as "dumb," "stupid," "airhead," etc.;
			6. have difficulty learning to tell time and prefer to wear a digital watch;
			7. chew on pencils, buttons, collars, or whatever is handy;
			8. find change threatening and have difficulty handling new situations;
			9. seem depressed.

Evaluation: All children display some of these signs and signals at times. The possibility that a student is in the wrong grade should be considered when the student consistently displays several signs or signals over an extended period of time. An example would be 3 or more signs or signals, occurring often for 2 or more weeks and increasingly interfering with the child's home, school, and social life.

9-Year-Olds: Signs and signals of wrong grade placement

NEVER
RARELY
OFTEN

At Home
A 9-year-old in the wrong grade may:

1. demand excessive assistance with homework, thus causing family tension;

2. express fear about going on to the next grade;

3. express concern about or try to avoid tests.

At School
A 9-year-old in the wrong grade may:

1. prefer playing with younger children;

2. often mix manuscript and cursive writing (some mixing is normal);

3. observe what is happening elsewhere in the classroom, rather than focusing on the work at hand;

4. complete only parts of assignments;

5. look for excuses to leave the classroom ("May I go to the lunch room and find out what's on the menu?");

6. be the last one chosen for team games and sports;

7. need to be taught the same concepts again and again—for example, he or she may need the rules of division, capitalization, and punctuation repeated frequently, and then will forget them again over the weekend or during a vacation period;

8. be unable to memorize the multiplication and/or division tables, and so need to keep sneaking peeks at the charts;

9. constantly break pencils, necessitating extra trips to the pencil sharpener;

10. be unable to locate pencils, pens, papers, and books in his or her own desk;

11. forget how to "set up" a paper with name, date, subject, and margins;

12. copy another child's work when under extreme pressure;

13. "trail" the teacher around the classroom;

14. have difficulty with test-prep activities and exhibit signs of test-related anxiety;

15. do work that is significantly below grade level in a number of subject areas.

NEVER	RARELY	OFTEN	**In General** **A 9-year-old in the wrong grade may:**
			1. need an abundance of supervision and reassurance;
			2. not work well independently;
			3. develop a preoccupation with "being right";
			4. procrastinate and avoid work;
			5. daydream frequently;
			6. develop a nervous tic—a twitching eye, a nervous cough, frequent clearing of the throat or twirling of hair;
			7. seem depressed.

Evaluation: All children display some of these signs and signals at times. The possibility that a student is in the wrong grade should be considered when the student consistently displays several signs or signals over an extended period of time. An example would be 3 or more signs or signals, occurring often for 2 or more weeks and increasingly interfering with the child's home, school, and social life.

10-Year-Olds: Signs and signals of wrong grade placement

(Column headers, diagonal: NEVER / RARELY / OFTEN)

At School
A 10-year-old in the wrong grade may:

			1. prefer to play with younger children;
			2. have great difficulty with abstractions in math, such as division, fractions, and geometry;
			3. enjoy playing with clay, erasers, rubber bands, and tape, and keep on the desk such "toys" as fancy erasers, homemade pencil holders, etc.;
			4. have difficulty shifting from one task to another;
			5. notice and welcome every distraction in the classroom—become a self-appointed reporter of flickering lights, hornets, changes in the weather, aromas from the lunch room, etc.;
			6. seem unable to work independently;
			7. function best under a rigid schedule;
			8. be the last one chosen for team games and sports;
			9. have difficulty following directions and frequently ask to have directions repeated;
			10. be unable to remember the multiplication and/or division tables, as well as other math facts;
			11. make a short story long—his or her skills as a storyteller delay having to get down to work;
			12. have difficulty with test-prep activities and exhibit signs of test-related anxiety;
			13. do work that is significantly below grade level in a number of subject areas.

In General
A 10-year-old in the wrong grade may:

			1. become passive;
			2. act defensively when reminded to finish work;
			3. develop a nervous tic—a twitching eye, a nervous cough, frequent clearing of the throat or twirling of hair;
			4. fear being promoted to the next grade;
			5. seem depressed.

Evaluation: All students display some of these signs and signals at times. The possibility that a student is in the wrong grade should be considered when the student consistently displays several signs or signals over an extended period of time. An example would be 3 or more signs or signals, occurring often for 2 or more weeks and increasingly interfering with the child's home, school, and social life.

11-Year-Olds: Signs and signals of wrong grade placement

NEVER
RARELY
OFTEN

At School
An 11-year-old in the wrong grade may:

			1. prefer to play with younger children;
			2. try to avoid cursive writing and ask permission to print (or try to negotiate: "If I write the first five sentences cursively, can I print the next five?");
			3. prefer using crayons instead of colored pencils, because crayons are easier to hold and use;
			4. toy with such items as pencils, fancy erasers, and scissors (he may discover that he can dismantle his pen and make it into a whistle);
			5. prefer white paper instead of yellow, because yellow tears more easily when she erases (which is constantly);
			6. want continual reassurance and checking of work ("Is this right?");
			7. choose individual rather than team sports;
			8. find many excuses for moving around the classroom—such as watering the plants—when it's time to write;
			9. frequently forget to bring in permission slips, absentee notes, lunch, musical instruments, etc.;
			10. write very brief reports;
			11. seldom if ever volunteer;
			12. become the self-appointed class timekeeper ("Ten more minutes until recess!");
			13. make excuses for work, such as claims that "I was never taught that in fifth grade";
			14. have a difficult time writing a report in his/her own words;
			15. produce challenging school work only when under constant pressure from parents and teacher;
			16. prefer "concrete" subjects and have difficulty understanding abstractions, such as concepts, relationships, or cause and effect;
			17. have difficulty with test-prep activities and exhibit signs of test-related anxiety;
			18. do work that is substantially below grade level in a variety of subject areas.

NEVER	RARELY	OFTEN	
			In General
			An 11-year-old in the wrong grade may:
			1. fear being promoted to the next grade;
			2. develop imaginary illnesses and injuries, such as a limp, bump, various aches, etc.;
			3. have a poor self-image and low self-esteem;
			4. write very small or very large;
			5. compare himself or herself negatively to other students;
			6. seem depressed;
			7. talk about running away.

Evaluation: All students display some of these signs and signals at times. The possibility that a student is in the wrong grade should be considered when the student consistently displays several signs or signals over an extended period of time. An example would be 3 or more signs or signals, occurring often for 2 or more weeks and increasingly interfering with the child's home, school, and social life.

Middle School: Signs and signals of wrong grade placement

NEVER RARELY OFTEN

At School
A middle school student in the wrong grade may:

			1. want to visit his or her previous grade;
			2. fall way behind with homework;
			3. act like a clown in class;
			4. complain that there is no recess;
			5. be confused about the daily schedule and about changing classes and teachers;
			6. have school notebooks that are nearly blank inside;
			7. become obsessed with a fear of going on to high school;
			8. drop the study of a musical instrument because of loss of interest;
			9. participate only passively in school activities—not become involved with plays, the yearbook, dances, contests, or any other extracurricular activities;
			10. focus exclusively on academics—seem unable to handle involvement both in school life and social life;
			11. have difficulty coping with departmentalization;
			12. display immature behavior at dances or while viewing some life education films/videos/materials;
			13. be promoted to high school on trial;
			14. begin to "act out" while riding on the school bus;
			15. have difficulty with abstract subjects such as algebra;
			16. have difficulty with test-prep activities and exhibit signs of test-related anxiety;
			17. do work that is significantly below grade level in a number of subject areas.

NEVER	RARELY	OFTEN	
			In General **A pre-adolescent or early adolescent in the wrong grade may:**
			1. procrastinate and/or manage time poorly;
			2. complain about nearly everything—school, the teacher, the school building, the other kids, life in general;
			3. lack motivation;
			4. begin to have discipline problems;
			5. play with younger children after school, on weekends, and during vacations;
			6. refuse to take direction from parents, yet be unable to make own choices;
			7. talk about suicide;
			8. exhibit an eating disorder;
			9. disturb the skin by picking, scratching, or cutting;
			10. pull hair out;
			11. feel inferior;
			12. talk about running away;
			13. begin to use alcohol or controlled substances;
			14. begin to experiment with or engage in sexual promiscuity;
			15. seem depressed.

Evaluation: All pre-adolescents and early adolescents display some of these signs and signals at times. The possibility that a student is in the wrong grade should be considered when the student consistently displays several signs or signals over an extended period of time. An example would be 3 or more signs or signals, occurring often for 2 or more weeks and increasingly interfering with the student's home, school, and social life.

High School: Signs and signals of wrong grade placement

NEVER
RARELY
OFTEN

At School
A teenager in the wrong grade may:

			1. have failing grades;
			2. not complete homework assignments;
			3. cause problems on the school bus in the afternoon—releasing tension built up during the day;
			4. cut classes and/or skip school frequently;
			5. refuse to make up work;
			6. do only enough to meet minimal requirements;
			7. not seek the extra help that's needed;
			8. have difficulty adapting to the senior high school schedule;
			9. produce work that does not reflect his or her innate ability;
			10. take only easy subjects;
			11. have difficulty with abstract subjects such as algebra;
			12. not participate in any extracurricular activities;
			13. have difficulty with test-prep activities and exhibit signs of test-related anxiety;
			14. do work that is significantly below grade level in a number of subject areas.

NEVER	RARELY	OFTEN	**In General** **A teenager in the wrong grade may:**
			1. complain constantly;
			2. use time unwisely;
			3. develop discipline problems, including aggressive or antisocial behavior;
			4. rely excessively on a mentor, such as a guidance counselor, nurse, or teacher;
			5. talk about dropping out of school and getting a job;
			6. become self-destructive—for example, start abusing alcohol or using controlled substances;
			7. neglect to inform parents of important matters, such as the dates of the SAT's or the deadline for an important scholarship application;
			8. begin to fight losing battles with authority figures;
			9. fantasize about suicide;
			10. exhibit an eating disorder;
			11. disturb the skin by picking, scratching, or cutting;
			12. pull hair out;
			13. feel inferior;
			14. talk about running away;
			15. engage in sexual promiscuity;
			16. seem depressed.

Evaluation: All adolescents display some of these signs and signals at times. The possibility that a student is in the wrong grade or program should be considered when the student consistently displays several signs or signals over an extended period of time. An example would be 3 or more signs or signals, occurring often for 2 or more weeks and increasingly interfering with the student's home, school, and social life.

85

College: Signs and signals of course overplacement (enrolling too young or taking courses that are too difficult)

NEVER
RARELY
OFTEN

At College
An overplaced college student may:

			1. receive poor grades;
			2. complain that he or she can't study because the dorm is too noisy (or too quiet);
			3. cut classes;
			4. complain about all the courses and all the professors;
			5. complain that college is "too easy" or "too boring";
			6. make self-destructive choices—for example, when it's time to study, he plays touch football, and then when the game's over, he goes out for a beer;
			7. spend time only on academics, participating in no extracurricular collegiate activities;
			8. never quite find a major;
			9. take or claim to have taken too many courses;
			10. have difficulty with abstract subjects;
			11. do work that does not meet course requirements in a number of subject areas;
			12. have difficulty with test-prep activities and exhibit signs of test-related anxiety;
			13. last only one semester and then quit.

In General
An overplaced college student may:

			1. call home constantly or come home every weekend;
			2. love to visit "my old high school" to keep "one foot in the high school camp";
			3. talk constantly of transferring to another college;
			4. flirt with the idea of quitting college and working or taking time off for a year;
			5. develop a strong interest in cults that offer a supportive, family-style environment;
			6. fantasize about suicide;
			7. exhibit an eating disorder;
			8. disturb the skin by picking, scratching, or cutting;
			9. feel inferior;
			10. pull out his or her hair;
			11. develop a dependence on alcohol or controlled substances;
			12. engage in sexual promiscuity;
			13. seem depressed.

Evaluation: All college students display some of these signs and signals at times. The possibility that a student is overplaced should be considered when the student consistently displays several signs or signals over an extended period of time. An example would be 3 or more signs or signals, occurring often for 2 or more weeks and increasingly interfering with the student's family, school, and social life.

CHAPTER 5

Evaluating Development: The Key to Correct Grade Placement

"It would be a fallacy to think all children are ready at the same time. 'Late bloomers' deserve to be identified and have their pace respected."
– T. Berry Brazelton, M.D., *Touchpoints.*

If you are concerned about a child's grade placement due to one of the checklists in the preceding chapter or for some other reason, what should you do next?

Keep learning.

A single checklist or assessment or standardized test or parent-teacher conference or neighbor's opinion or article or book (including this one) or any other individual indicator should *never* be the *sole* basis for making a grade placement decision. Instead, a concerned parent or teacher should amass *numerous* sources of information and feedback, which can then be combined with any "gut feelings" and a caring, common-sense determination to do what is best for the particular student in question.

The main reason that numerous sources of information and feedback are needed is that determining whether a struggling student is in the wrong grade is not an exact science. There is no infallible formula or crystal ball that provides quick and easy answers. But just as a "preponderance of evidence" can be the deciding factor in a legal case (which, unfortunately, is what too many education issues are becoming), multiple sources of information and feedback can usually provide a reasonable basis for making a difficult grade placement decision.

Compiling this information should also demonstrate to (and reassure) all those involved that a thorough and thoughtful approach to this critical decision is being used, as opposed to the standard official method of counting birthday candles on some arbitrarily selected day.

So if you're going to take your responsibility seriously and do the job right, what information should be sought and considered while preparing to make a grade placement decision?

Some of the factors and circumstances mentioned in preceding chapters—such as chronological age, gender, previous or current health issues, any preschool and school records (including attendance data)—are fairly straightforward and often easy to ascertain and interpret. There is, however, another crucial factor that may prove more difficult to identify precisely, even though it often seems readily apparent to experienced educators and insightful parents. This vital factor is the child's individual rate and process of development, which results in the child's current developmental stage.

What is a "developmental stage"?

A child's developmental stage is the level at which the child is functioning as a total human being, including his or her hands, eyes, muscles, bones, nervous system, and brain. A school-age student at a particular stage of development can perform certain tasks with skill and ease, but the same student will not be able to perform certain other tasks well until further biological development (including neurological development) occurs.

Developmental stages may not correspond exactly to children's chronological ages. Children go through predictable stages of development that are similar for every healthy, normal child, but the timing of these stages can vary widely. In fact, many experts believe that a child can be as much as a year ahead of or behind the chronological average and still be considered normal. These variations are compounded by schools' reliance on a single, arbitrary grade placement cut-off date, which results in some students not only being much younger chronologically than others in their class but also being developmentally young as well.

Most parents recognize that every child does not reach the same level of development at exactly the same age as every other child. And most parents also recognize the futility of trying to control variations in development. You cannot simply tell a child, "Okay, Johnny, Sam started walking when he was one year old. Today you turned one, so start walking." Of course, a parent can try this approach, but what happens next is probably a better lesson for the parent than the child. Life simply does not work this way.

Variations in development continue throughout the early childhood years. Jean may begin talking at 11 months and Janet at 21 months, and both are developing their speaking abilities within a normal, perfectly acceptable time span for children. Of course, if a test of verbal language were to be administered to each child at 18 months, Jean would do well and Janet would flunk, but in all likelihood both children are fine and developing exactly as they should. Grown-ups' expectations may have changed in recent years, but most children's innate capabilities and patterns of development have not.

Similar variations continue throughout the primary grades, intermediate grades, middle school, and high school. Students who have reached different developmental stages start reading at different times, mastering other skills at different times, grasping abstract concepts at different times, and so on. While an individual student's timetable is clearly affected by his or her previous experiences, as well as what and how he or she is being taught, it is also profoundly affected by the internal biological processes that are proceeding quite independently of anyone's desires, hopes, expectations, standards, or mandates.

The critical importance and uncontrollable nature of children's developmental stages tend to be better understood and respected during a child's first years of life. After that, however, these same vital processes tend to be ignored (often with dire consequences) as the young children become students and continue to develop at different rates and paces. Even though some parents now try to "jumpstart" their babies and toddlers, most parents still recognize that different children start crawling at different times, teething at different times, walking at different times, and talking at different times. But once children turn five, somehow they are all expected to be ready for the same educational experience at the same time—and able to complete it in the same amount of time.

"Research confirms common sense. Some students take three to six times longer than others to learn the same thing. Yet students are caught in a time trap— processed on an assembly line schedule to the minute. Our usage of time virtually assures the failure of many students."
– Report of the National Education Commission on Time and Learning, 1994.

Development is not a contest

The reality is that a child who talks at an early age is not superior to a child who talks several months later. In all likelihood, the child who starts talking later will reach all the same stages as the child who talked sooner. And the child who talked later may also, in fact, become a far better talker (and student and worker) than the one who talked first.

When it comes to sending their children to school and considering grade placement, however, parents sometimes ignore what their own common sense and experience tell them. On one level, they may realize that Rob or Susie or Steve or Sally would benefit from additional time to develop, or from being placed in a grade better matched to their current stage of development. Yet some parents may still end up denying the evidence before their eyes and not trusting their own judgment, because of concern about others' opinions or because they think proceeding at a slower pace will somehow put their child at a competitive disadvantage. In fact, the student at a competitive disadvantage is the one who is developmentally too young for a particular grade or program, rather than one who has previously taken the time needed to develop and succeed.

First grade, for example, requires a student to have the ability to concentrate despite distractions and to cope with a full day at school. First grade also requires coordination between the hands and eyes, so that the student can write words on a page. A student who has not reached the developmental stage needed to meet these requirements is at risk and may fail first grade, no matter how intelligent that student is.

While much has been done to make the primary grades developmentally appropriate in recent years, there are now strong pressures to increase the amount and level of formal academic instruction. In addition to the pressures created by politicians and some education "experts," pressure may also come from parents who think that speeding up a student's academic progress is advantageous, regardless of how the child is developing as a human being.

As students move up through the grades, what was once a small gap between grade-level standards and a student's developmental stage can soon turn into an unfathomable abyss. Once students reach third and fourth grade, for example, they are increasingly expected to:

- use cursive handwriting
- memorize multiplication and division tables
- comprehend abstract mathematics
- read expository text
- spell correctly
- complete independent work
- write book reports and extended essays
- pass standardized tests.

Of course, the vast majority of students do develop the ability to handle this advanced curriculum. They just don't all do it at the same time, and if any grown-ups really think all students can or should, those grown-ups have some further development of their own to do. Unfortunately, one of the major problems in education today is that there are many such grown-ups in our state legislatures, departments of education, schools, and communities. And one result of their unreasonable expectations is a substantial increase in what middle and high school educators now refer to as "D.O.A."—Deficit On Arrival. In other words, many incoming students have not yet succeeded in mastering the knowledge and skills they need to meet upper-grade standards.

The whole child goes to school

If you listen to some of those developmentally challenged grown-ups, you might think that intelligence and academic performance are the only criteria for school success. Simply stuffing a student's head with words and numbers—and providing extensive computer training—might seem like the primary responsibility of today's schools.

For better or worse, students are not robots who can be fed information that is then stored, processed, and spit out in different ways. Pressuring students of any age to learn material they cannot yet understand or apply to other areas of the curriculum is a self-defeating exercise. The real lesson being taught is that pleasing clueless adults is the top priority, and since the students cannot really succeed in doing this anyhow, why bother?

"Too many parents—and teachers—get great pleasure from watching a 4-year-old count to 50. But what good does that do when the child has no concept of what 50 is? Even a parrot can mimic numbers."
– Harold Jaus, Associate Professor of Education at Purdue University, quoted in *The New York Times.*

Students are complex human beings—not memory storage units—and they need to develop their physical, social, and emotional capabilities, as well as their intellectual capabilities. As indicated earlier, attempts to speed up or overemphasize intellectual development not only fail to educate a student effectively, they may also backfire and actually lead to poor performance in school. Even if successful, such efforts can also result in a student who is developmentally out of balance—a student in danger of failing to achieve the emotional satisfaction and healthy social relationships that are also vital components of success in school and in life.

This problem can be compounded by the fact that a child does not necessarily mature in all areas of development at the same rate. It is not unusual, for example, to see a student function intellectually at the level of a 7-year-old, but when the student's physical, social, and emotional capabilities are factored in, the overall developmental stage is more like that of a 5-year-old.

A common-sense approach to school readiness and grade placement therefore requires adults to consider all four aspects of development. The following sections of this chapter look in more detail at some key considerations in regard to each of these areas.

School success includes having a friend

When children first walk into a classroom at the start of a new school year, what do you think their primary concern is? If you think they are worrying only about reading and writing—or any other academic matter—think again.

Having or not having a friend is extremely important for students of all ages. Young children are going to be separated from their parents and any other personal caregiver for an extended period of time every day, so their standing with their peer group is becoming much more significant than it was in the past. And as students move up through the grades, social relationships tend to take on even greater importance, which is why the social aspects of a child's developmental stage are a very important consideration in grade placement decisions.

A parent who has had to watch while his or her child was left out of a group will know just how painful school can be for a student too young to fit in. Preschool experiences and parental "coaching" can help with some aspects of a young child's social development, but a student who remains at a younger developmental stage as the years go by will become well aware of the difference, as will the student's classmates. And because the primary grades are a particularly important period in the development of a child's self-image, frequent feelings of rejection or inferiority can have serious and long-lasting consequences.

For older students, playing with siblings or parents is usually not sufficient. Friends in the same class or grade tend to become a vital source of support, recreation, and satisfaction. On the other hand, not having friends can upset and distract a student—and even lead to the perception that he or she is a misfit or failure.

School success and happiness are inter-related

Is a child emotionally ready for a particular grade or program? Can a young boy really share "his" teacher with all the other kids? Will primary grade girls be traumatized while riding on the school bus with upper elementary or middle school giants who are saying and doing things that the younger students may not yet be ready to handle? Is a student of any age ready to handle the increasingly stressful classroom demands created by a diverse student population, an advanced curriculum linked to high standards, and intensive test-prep drills?

Some young children become upset when another child is scolded, as if being in trouble is contagious. When a little girl comes home from school with her bottom lip curled and quivering, Mom picks up the body language and asks, "What happened?" Sally might answer, "Rob got yelled at today. He was sitting just two seats away from me. Maybe next time she'll come over and yell at me."

Older students may become unhappy about social or family problems, and the unhappiness and related distraction can then lead to academic problems. Or academic problems may become the cause—not the effect—of unhappiness and family problems. Worst of all, a vicious cycle may develop in which emotional and academic problems swirl together and become virtually inseparable, constantly undermining efforts by the student and others to "sort things out" and "get back on track."

School success depends on physical development

The physical strain that young students experience in school can be considerable, but at least it is usually obvious. As students proceed through the grades, many grown-ups tend to assume that a student's success or failure is simply a matter of hard work and intellectual ability, which are now totally independent of physical processes such as hand-eye coordination or the development of the brain. The truth, of course, is very different.

If you can remember what it was like to learn to read (few people can), or if you have recently watched a student go through this process, you know that it takes tremendous energy to concentrate young eyes and brains on recognizing letters, combining them into a word, and then understanding that word in the context of all the preceding and following words.

And consider the contortions a first grader goes through when learning to write. He may squeeze his pencil so tightly that his fingertips turn white, while his neck and shoulder muscles may become visibly tense. The girl sitting next to him may have her tongue sticking out of the side of her mouth and moving, to help the writing process along. This happens because learning to write involves the entire child in the very difficult task of coordinating mind and muscles in a way never done before. After fifteen or twenty minutes, the child is usually exhausted. And after a five-and-a-quarter-hour day in school, many young students urgently need a nap.

Of course, older students are expected to be beyond all that as they go through the process of learning cursive writing, which is usually taught in third grade precisely because drawing slanted lines and connections correctly is physically more challenging. And what's so physical about completing a multiplication quiz correctly, other than using your eyes to identify each number in sequence, using your nervous system to transmit data to and from the brain, remembering or working out the answer within your brain, and then using your hand to write each answer legibly and quickly?

Some technological visionaries think that teaching keyboarding skills at an early age is the answer to some of these physical challenges. But small third graders still have trouble reaching all the keys. And quick keyboarding creates its own physical demands on the eyes, brain, nervous system, and fingers. Hopefully, most people still recognize that creating students capable only of pointing and clicking with a mouse would be an educational failure of huge proportions.

Perhaps sometime soon we'll see a newsflash announcing that recent research on the brain has confirmed that it remains a physical part of students' bodies. Meanwhile, it seems safe to assume that the physical development of the brain and other key body parts has a direct effect on students' ability to learn and perform in the classroom. So students whose physical development is proceeding more slowly may be at a severe disadvantage academically.

School success blends with intellectual/academic development

Distinguishing between the physical development of the brain and a child's intellectual/academic development is not easy, but there is at least one important difference. The physical development of the brain is difficult to measure, because the brain is still not fully understood and accessible. Intellectual/academic development, in contrast, can be relatively easy to identify and measure, based primarily on a student's verbal, drawn, or written output.

Whatever that output is—and however it is measured—the key point for educators and parents to remember is that virtually every child is ready to learn something. Students achieve success in school when what they learn and how they are taught match their current stage of development. Students sink below grade level and become increasingly at risk for failure when they are not yet ready for the curriculum and methods of instruction being used in their classes.

Parents and educators therefore must make sure that the curriculum and methods of instruction are neither too challenging nor too easy for a student at a particular stage of intellectual/academic development. And when a student consistently does below-grade work in a number of subject areas for an extended period of time, responsible parents and educators must consider the possibility that the student is not yet ready for the grade-level curriculum and methods of instruction, much less any requisite statewide tests for that grade.

Parents, in particular, also need to remember that a student's intellectual/academic development is not a measure of intelligence. Nor is it a race. As in the fable of the tortoise and the hare, experienced educators know that some bright, driven, early achievers grow disinterested and "burnt out" in the upper grades after being pushed too hard too soon, while many "late bloomers" go on to demonstrate tremendous intelligence and achieve great success after being given the additional time they need to develop and learn.

"As decisions about preschool, kindergarten, and first grade arise, the following reasons to give children extra time should be considered:

Family patterns of slow development—'late bloomers'
Prematurity or physical problems in early life
Immature motor development—awkwardness, poor motor skills, such as in catching or throwing a ball, drawing, or cutting
Easy distractibility and short attention span
Difficulty with right-left hand or eye-hand coordination, such as in copying a circle or diamond
Lagging social development—difficulty taking turns, sharing, or playing. If the child is shunned by children her own age, take it seriously.

Each of these might be a reason to allow a child to mature another year before starting preschool, or to stay in preschool or kindergarten a year longer."
– T. Berry Brazelton, M.D., *Touchpoints.*

Evaluating a young child's development

If you have concerns about a young child's readiness for a particular grade or program, how can you identify the child's current developmental stage in order to place the child in the right grade or program, thereby providing the best opportunity for school success right from the start?

Evaluating young children's developmental readiness can be a challenge, because their academic output and school experiences are preliminary at best—and may even be nonexistent. There are also wide variations in children's *rate* of development at this point, so sudden advances or periods of consolidation may occur. Moreover, children at this age are not good at taking tests, so the wrong sort of assessment may actually measure the child's ability to take the test rather than the child's current stage of development.

For about fifty years, however, educators and other experts on early childhood have successfully used evaluation tools known as "developmental assessments" or "school readiness screening examinations" to provide information about a young child's current stage of development. These evaluations measure such things as a child's motor skills, coordination, attention span, visual perception, clarity of speech, ability to follow directions, and ability to sustain a function—all important elements of early school success.

There are no wrong answers in this sort of evaluation, as it simply helps to identify the child's current stage so that an appropriate program placement decision can be made. It is also quite different from an I.Q. test or reading readiness test, neither of which provides information about a child's overall developmental level. Most children actually enjoy participating in a developmental assessment, because it uses age-appropriate techniques and focuses on what a child can do.

These sorts of evaluations are based on extensive research that includes long and careful observation of thousands of children of various ages. The best-known and most popular are the Gesell Developmental Assessments, which grew out of the work of Dr. Arnold Gesell, a professor at Yale University who devoted much of his work to the study of child development. Most other evaluation tools of this sort are patterned after the Gesell Assessments and borrow from Dr. Gesell's pioneering research on children's ages and stages.

The information provided by a developmental assessment or school readiness screening should always be combined with other information based on parents' and teachers' observations, in order to make an accurate grade placement decision. Parents can provide important information about a child's prior development, which can help explain and confirm evaluation results. Teachers can utilize their years of experience observing children in group situations, as well as their firsthand knowledge of whatever educational programs are available. Through the use of all this information, parents and educators working together can make the best possible decisions for the children in their care.

Is the developmental assessment or screening examination below grade?

It is important to remember that not every screening instrument used to evaluate children developmentally is readiness-oriented. Schools screen and test children for a variety of reasons, such as trying to determine specific academic abilities or identify children who are considered "culturally disadvantaged," "educationally handicapped," "gifted," etc. An instrument designed for these purposes is fundamentally different from a developmental readiness screening examination.

Other assessments may claim to evaluate a child's development but not actually do so effectively. The following checklist will help you to understand and recognize effective school readiness screening examinations:

Readiness Evaluation Checklist

Eleven Vital Characteristics of an Effective
Developmental Readiness Screening Examination

1. The examination is individually administered.
2. The examiner has achieved a required professional standard of training.
3. The examination measures the "whole" child, including the emotional, social, physical, and intellectual aspects of development.
4. The examination is not culturally, linguistically, or economically biased.
5. The examination is not weighted heavily on language development.
6. The examination has proven to be valid and reliable, based on research compiled by the school or other education organizations.
7. The examination follows a stated philosophical point of view based on established principles of child development.
8. The process by which a child completes a task is as important or more important than the task itself.
9. All answers are correct for the respondent.
10. No child ever "fails."
11. The examination provides a score or range designed to be used for a program or grade placement recommendation, and to match the curriculum to the child.

Evaluating an older student's developmental readiness

As students begin to emerge from the primary grades, much more evidence is available. But sorting through it and reaching the right conclusions can still be challenging.

First and foremost, parents and educators must remember to consider all four areas of development, not just the intellectual/academic realm. Teachers, guidance counselors, and/or school psychiatrists should be able to provide information about a student's social, emotional, and physical development, all of which may help to explain—and will definitely provide an important context for considering—a student's intellectual/academic development.

In addition to any report cards, portfolios of work, standardized test scores, and evaluations by teachers and/or school psychologists, an "individual skills inventory" can provide valuable information about a student's current capabilities. There are also books, such as *Yardsticks* by Chip Wood, that provide more general guidelines about what can be expected at a particular age.

But when evaluating an older student's intellectual/academic development, it is also important to remember that there may be a huge gap between current curriculum standards and traditional developmental standards. In many states, a politically driven determination to raise academic standards has resulted in state legislators and bureaucrats making decisions that do not take into account normal variations in child development, much less any individual needs or special circumstances. And statewide tests designed to hold schools accountable may be "driving" the curriculum even faster and further, leaving the capabilities of a significant number of students far behind.

As a result, a 9-year-old who traditionally would have been seen as developing at a slower but still normal rate may now have great difficulty with an advanced 4th grade curriculum that includes intensive preparation for a high-stakes standardized test. And rather than insist that the student, teacher, parents, and school all make major adjustments in order to help the student "squeak by" with below-grade work, a wiser course of action may be to give this still-young child another year to develop and learn, after which above-grade work and high test scores could well follow.

Readiness for what?

When making grade placement decisions based on developmental readiness evaluation results and other input, remember that the most important question is not *whether* a student is ready for a particular grade or program. Rather, the key question is *which* grade or program the student is ready for. Responsible educators recognize that every child is ready for some sort of learning experience, so schools should provide options that meet different children's needs. With this in mind, developmental readiness evaluations can help to ensure that schools are ready for their full range of students, rather than trying (unsuccessfully) to force all students to master the same "one-size-fits-all" curriculum at the same time.

Whoever coined the phrase "nothing succeeds like success" had a good understanding of how students, as well as adults, achieve. In addition to providing needed knowledge and skills, school success creates the confidence and positive attitudes that lead to more success. When young children are provided with educational experiences for which they are ready, they succeed in learning and then are intellectually and emotionally ready for challenging new learning experiences. These children become students who learn well and enjoy the process.

In contrast, consider the plight of a late bloomer who struggles through initial school experiences for which the child is *not* yet ready. Intellectually and academically, this student probably has not mastered the concepts and skills needed for the next stage of the learning process. Emotionally, this student is likely to have negative feelings about school, based both on previous experience and on the recognition that he or she is not well prepared for the more challenging learning experiences ahead. Socially, this student may be having difficulty making and keeping friends, because he or she does not have the same skills and maturity as many classmates. Physically, this student may tend to be bullied and picked last for teams, as well as be unable to perform certain concrete or conceptual tasks, all of which further undermine success in other areas of development.

Not only is a situation like this likely to result in below-grade performance, it also just plain unfair and harmful for any young person. And it is especially unfair and harmful for a student who is actually a hard worker, a smart thinker, and a good kid, but who is just developing somewhat more slowly and therefore not yet ready for a particular grade or program.

This is exactly the sort of situation that some schools successfully avoid by providing options that enable students to obtain additional growing and learning time, before they begin to struggle and fail. In the next chapter, we'll explore some of these successful options and see how they can help students achieve success before any long-lasting damage occurs.

CHAPTER 6

Getting Schools Ready for Their Students

When I graduated from Keene State College in 1967, I found a job teaching a 5th/6th grade multiage class in a small, rural community in New Hampshire. My first year as a teacher was a tremendous experience, and I felt I had achieved a lot of success. When I went back for my second year, the Assistant Superintendent of Schools came to see me. He said, "Jim, we're pleased with you, and we want to give you a chance to experience upward mobility. We're going to make you Principal of the Temple Elementary School."

"Well," I said, "I may not look very bright, but I am gifted in math, and I know that would make me Temple's fifth principal in twenty-four months. I'm not sure I can stand that kind of upward mobility." In spite of my reservations, when I woke up the following Monday, I was the principal of an elementary school.

The teacher of the first grade class presented me with my first challenge. "I don't know what I'm going to do with my twenty-five children," she said. "They're all over the place. I have trouble getting them to focus long enough for me to teach them anything."

I went to her classroom, opened the door, and quickly closed it again from the hallway. Nothing in my teacher education classes or one year of actual teaching experience had prepared me to deal with what I saw.

It was then that I brought in my former teacher, Nancy Richard, as an early childhood consultant who could advise me on the students' development and education. She observed the class and said, "What you really have in that room are first graders doing second grade work, first graders doing first grade work, first graders doing kindergarten work, first graders doing no work at all, and then there are those two boys in the corner who aren't toilet trained after lunch."

"Some of these children," she continued, "aren't ready to do first grade work yet. Chronologically, they are 6, but developmentally they are still too young to succeed in that class." She then suggested that I take a course on developmental ages and stages.

In that course, I was surprised to learn that up to 25% of the students in American schools repeat a grade, and as many as another 25% are often struggling and not succeeding in their current grade. I checked the registers covering a six-year period at my school and proved those statistics were flawed. In my school, 33% of the kids had repeated! This informal survey also showed that most of the students who repeated were boys, and the grade most students repeated was first grade.

Being a bright, young, "overplaced" principal, I immediately made two brilliant deductions: boys are stupid, and first grade teachers are incompetent. Further reflection, observation, and discussion led me to some different conclusions, however. I began to consider the possibility that girls tended to develop more rapidly in certain respects than boys, and that these differences reached the crisis point in first grade, when all the students were somehow expected to learn how to read and write at the same time.

One September in the late 1960s, we began screening and observing children to help determine their developmental readiness for a first grade experience. We discovered that many of the children eligible for first grade on the basis of their age that year were at risk for school failure when placed in a traditional first grade program. After I shared that news with their parents and recommended that the developmentally young children remain in kindergarten for another year, the parents were very unhappy. They decided to send all of those late-blooming children into first grade as a single group, thinking that the children being together would somehow make a difference in their ability to succeed in first grade.

Of course it did not. By the middle of October, several of the children had been withdrawn from first grade at their parents' request and moved back to kindergarten. The problems that were surfacing at home and at school made the parents realize that these children really did need more time to grow and prepare for first grade. The rest of the developmentally young students ended up taking two years to complete first grade.

The next year, when we assessed the entering children's developmental levels, we did more to inform the parents—at PTO meetings, in one-on-one meetings, through books and handouts. That year many children who were developmentally young stayed in kindergarten for an additional year of growing and learning time, and then they entered first grade when most of them were 7 years old. That first group of children, who had the advantage of an additional year, graduated from high school in 1982, and many went on to graduate from college in 1986.

Nationwide, thousands of schools also began providing developmentally young children with an additional year of growing and learning time during the 1960s, helping tens of thousands of students master the curriculum and achieve success in school. This concept, which was first formulated in 1911 and later formalized as a Title III government program in New Hampshire in 1966, spread rapidly as teachers and parents recognized firsthand how much some students benefited from having an additional year to develop and learn *before* they experienced years of frustration and failure in school. Numerous research studies done during the following decades showed that this approach helped many students improve their performance and their attitude.

More than three decades after my initial teaching experiences, the range of students in most classrooms has grown even more diverse, and in many cases their needs are more intense and complex. At the same time, a more advanced curriculum driven by high standards, combined with intensive test preparation to help students cope with high-stakes examinations, have "raised the bar" and therefore put at risk some additional students who probably would have been allowed to "scrape by" in earlier decades. Under these circumstances, there is a greater need than ever for options that provide an additional year of growing and learning time to struggling learners, who may not yet be ready to succeed in the particular grade to which they have been assigned.

"I would contend that much of today's school failure results from academic expectations for which students' brains were not prepared—but which were bulldozed into them anyway."
– Jane M. Healy, Ph.D., *Endangered Minds.*

Ready or Not?

One kindergarten teacher told me this story:

"When pressure to meet state standards led to a requirement that kindergarten children be taught reading, a watered-down first grade reading program was introduced into the half-day kindergarten. Many of the children were not yet ready for this program, but the school board decided that the half-day time constraint was the reason the program didn't work. So they extended kindergarten to a full day, but most 5-year-olds still had problems with the reading program, and now they had an additional problem—many could not handle a full day of school that included this sort of work. The school board then appointed a study committee to investigate the merits of implementing a mandatory program for 4-year-olds. In other words, rather than providing appropriate work for each grade level, the push for early reading started turning preschool and kindergarten into prep schools for first grade!"

Of course there are ways to help *prepare* young children to learn to read, and a few four- and five-year-olds may actually be ready to learn to read, but some grown-ups still seem to think that setting extremely high standards and "pushing down" an advanced curriculum into a lower grade will force all the students to learn successfully. A more realistic scenario is that some students will rise to the occasion, while many more—including many developmentally young children and other differently able learners—will descend into the frustration, negative attitudes, and lack of mastery that often lead to outright failure. This is a particular problem in the primary grades, where students are forming their first impressions of school and of themselves as learners, and where many educators and parents have learned the hard way that an overly academic approach requires teaching in ways that are out of sync with the needs of young children.

"A child who is eager and ready for kindergarten and first grade is likely to become a lifelong learner. A child who is pushed to do too much too soon will never really like school and is likely to have problems all the way through. These are your child's formative years, and starting school should be a positive, rewarding experience."
– Judy Keshner, *Starting School.*

In the primary grades, students need learning experiences that are direct and hands-on, because most young children are not fully capable of understanding abstract concepts until they are older. For example, when taught math and science using objects they can actually feel, move, and see, young children learn far better than when they are asked to work only with abstract symbols such as words and numerals.

Students also benefit when they learn to read using a variety of colorful and interesting books, rather than just "basal readers" that may have limited subject matter and limited appeal. When learning to write, children gain knowledge and confidence by going through a "publishing" process that includes editing and correcting their work, then sharing it with others by reading it aloud. This process allows students to use "invented" or "temporary" spelling initially, so as not to detract from their desire to learn or from their confidence, but also encourages them to learn correct spelling in an appropriate, supportive way.

Other effective teaching techniques include the use of "themes" to integrate different subjects through the exploration of multi-faceted topics; and the use of "learning centers," where children can work together on specific projects or subjects, rather than having to sit at the same desk all day and listen while the teacher talks. Vast numbers of primary grade teachers now use combinations of "best practices" such as these, thereby helping students learn well and develop positive attitudes about school and themselves.

Unfortunately, during the early 1990s some educational extremists went so far as to claim that the use of these practices would eliminate the need for any student to have a year of additional learning time. Once schools had a "developmentally appropriate" curriculum, the theory went, variations in development and learning rates would even out by the time the children reached third grade. And until children reached this magical stage, classroom teachers could simply individualize the curriculum so that not a single child—anywhere in the United States—would ever fail or need an additional year to master the curriculum.

Of course, the proponents of this theory (mostly university professors, along with some state education officials) have never been able to identify a single school where this actually occurred. And third grade teachers at schools across America tend to break into either laughter or tears when told that all the students in their classes should now be catching up with each other and learning successfully. Because this never happened, the theory was later revised by some to say that all the students would catch up in fourth grade (this has been called "developmental inflation"), but obviously the real problem with the theory was not when it would happen, but the idea that it would ever happen at all.

In fact, this failed theory and its supporters are, in many ways, responsible for the current emphasis on high standards and high-stakes testing. The fact that young learners were being "passed along" from grade to grade each year without having learned vital information and skills resulted in huge deficits and other problems that surfaced in the upper elementary grades, middle school, and high school. This, in turn, led to pressure to introduce grade-level standards and then require students to demonstrate mastery by passing standardized tests before being allowed to proceed into the upper grades. This trend, in turn, resulted in many third and fourth grade classes resorting to high-pressure test preparation, for which many of the students who were supposed to catch up with everyone are still not ready.

Curriculum and time are two separate issues

In fact, there is no "magic" curriculum or grouping of students that will prevent children from continuing to develop at different rates. A 6-year-old who is developmentally too young to read will be unable to comprehend how our written language works in even the most interesting and colorful children's book. But given an extra year to grow and learn in a supportive educational environment, that same student will probably be ready, willing, and

111

able to read. This has been shown to be true in schools across America and is also just plain common sense—something notice-ably lacking in too many academic theories.

Interestingly, this approach has also been proven effective in many foreign countries, where the teaching of reading often oc-curs at a later age. And while critics of American schools have been quick to cite the low scores of American students in some international competitions, the same critics have been far less ea-ger to acknowledge and embrace the different educational prac-tices that result in the foreigners' higher scores.

"Cross-cultural studies also demonstrate the negative effects of early formal instruction and the benefits of appropriate practice...France has a state-mandated kindergarten reading program, and some 30 percent of the children have reading problems. However, in Denmark, a country with a high (almost 100 percent) literacy rate, formal instruction is not introduced until the second grade...[Russia], England, and Israel have adopted a similar approach and timetable."
– Anthony Coletta, Ph.D., *What's Best for Kids.*

The hard realities facing American students, parents and teachers today make additional growing and learning time even more nec-essary—not less necessary—than it has been in the past. The pressure to meet state standards and prepare students for high-stakes tests has prevented many teachers from providing the types of instruction that meet the needs of their diverse student popu-lations. Yet even when most students speak the same language, have similar backgrounds and capabilities, and come from rela-tively affluent families, many of the students are now less pre-pared to learn than in previous decades, due to factors such as changing parenting styles and overexposure to media.

These factors have contributed to an increase in the number of students who are less willing or able to accept grown-ups' author-ity, to get along peacefully with their classmates, and to focus on print for extended periods of time. As a result, discipline—rather than instruction—takes up too much of the school day, even when only a few disruptive students are in the classroom. This makes the classroom much less conducive to learning and, in extreme cases, forces the teacher to spend far too much time acting like a social worker or even a cop, instead of an educator.

As a result of all these trends, the refusal to provide an additional year of growing and learning time can set up both students and teachers for failure in today's accountability-driven education system. Students who are struggling in the wrong grade or program need extensive help just to get by, much less master an advanced curriculum. And when so many students are in need and teachers are so over-burdened, extensive and effective assistance is very unlikely to be provided to every student. But even in those very rare situations where such assistance is delivered, some students will still need an additional year to learn and grow in order to overcome natural variations in development, as well as the effects of being chronologically younger or other disadvantages such as poverty and limited English proficiency.

"When children face a school environment that is too sophisticated and busy for their current stage of development, they start to see themselves as being incapable of doing anything right. This is where the pattern of failure begins, and it may never go away."
– Judy Keshner, *Starting School.*

Fortunately, many schools now offer alternatives that enable these sorts of learners to become the successful students they can and should be. By providing an additional year to learn and grow in a supportive, continuous-progress program, schools help these students develop the intellectual, physical, social, and emotional capabilities needed to meet high grade-level standards. In many cases, the students become confident learners who excel academically and in other ways—instead of doing below-grade work and remaining trapped in the wrong grade.

Providing choice within a school

Options that provide students with an additional year of continuous-progress learning and growing time have many different names, but they share a number of important features. There are reasonable class sizes and a curriculum that is well matched to the current needs and capabilities of the students. This curriculum is also fully compatible with the curriculum in any preceding or following grades, so that students build on what they have previously learned and then can apply their knowledge and skills effectively in upper-level grades.

Another important feature is the widespread recognition that these classes are not a form of failure or grade-level retention. Rather, they are a form of early academic intervention designed to *prevent* failure and grade-level retention from occurring. There should also be a widespread recognition that these classes are a vital means of providing choice *within* a school. Instead of diverting students and funding elsewhere, these classes offer alternatives that help schools meet the needs of the full range of learners found in today's classrooms.

Readiness classes for "Young 5's"

Many primary and elementary schools find that significant numbers of entering students are not yet ready to succeed in today's kindergarten programs. This may be due to a child's innate but still normal rate of development, or due to other factors that have left the child unprepared to handle the more advanced curriculum and instruction now found in many kindergarten classes. Readiness classes provide the time needed to grow and proceed into the primary school environment in a supportive way, which then makes kindergarten a much more positive and educational experience. This is particularly important because, as kindergarten teacher Judy Keshner explains in her booklet, *Starting School*, kindergarten "is not a preview of what is to come—it is the foundation on which the following years will grow. Each grade builds on the one that came before, and kindergarten sets the pattern and the tone."

Transition classes (also known as half grades, bridge classes, etc.)

Call these what you will, this approach to providing an additional year of continuous-progress learning and growing time has been adopted at a variety of grade levels by schools across America. Essentially, these classes enable students to move on to a new room, a new teacher, and a new curriculum, but one that helps them complete what was started during the previous school year, while also better preparing them for what will come in the year that follows. This combination of additional time and well-matched curriculum and instruction can enable a struggling below-grade learner to become a fully capable above-grade student.

Following is a description of some of the levels at which these classes can prove particularly effective:

- Even though a growing number of public elementary schools are providing their own "pre-kindergarten" classes as an alternative to private preschools, some pre-k students are still likely to need an additional year to learn and grow before succeeding in kindergarten.
- Many schools have used "pre-first" classes to help at-risk 6-year-olds make the very difficult and important transition from the more child-oriented learning of kindergarten to the increasingly academic tasks emphasized in first grade.
- Transition classes can be used effectively before or after fifth grade, eighth grade, or whatever other grade is the "last chance" before facing the high-stakes tests and major transitions often required for middle school or high school.

"...as shown by the many studies in this book—a good number of which have been published in professional journals—high-quality extra-year programs can

*be quite effective in **reducing** the number of students who need remedial services, who are retained in the same grade, and who develop other characteristics which make them 'at-risk for dropping out.'"*
– *Real Facts from Real Schools* by James Uphoff, Ed.D.

Multiage classes

Schools nationwide now offer multiage classrooms in which students of different ages work and learn together, staying together with the same teacher for a multi-year placement. These classrooms reduce the wasted time and artificial constraints that result from having a new teacher and high-stakes pass/fail decisions every year.

Multiage classes make more time available for teaching and learning at the start of the year in particular, because teachers and students don't have to spend as much time getting to know one another and learning to work well together. The multiage approach also eliminates worries about "running out of time" to complete the curriculum by the end of each year. And it can eliminate some of the high-stakes decisions that otherwise would have to be made. For example, if a student needs an additional year to develop and complete the curriculum before facing a high-stakes test and either moving on or being held back, a multiage class can be especially beneficial, because it already contains a wide range of age levels and a flexible timetable rather than a rigid, lock-step grade structure.

Multiage classrooms can therefore decrease the risk of failure for all learners, because these classes allow students to develop and learn at their own rate in a much less hurried environment. Staying in the same class with the same teacher and classmates for more than one year also provides a sense of consistency and belonging, which can be particularly helpful for the many students who now grow up in fast-changing families and communities. And the developmental diversity that naturally occurs in a multiage classroom makes it easier for transfer and special-needs students to be included in them. Another important benefit is that all these types of learners can work closely with and learn from more experienced students during their first year, then become the models for new students during their second year.

One type of multiage class that works particularly well at the start of the primary grades is known as a Readiness/First Grade (R/1) Configuration. This approach acknowledges the reality that continues to exist in most first grade classes—students who need additional learning and growing time are blended with those who are truly ready for first grade. What makes the R/1 Configuration different is that the parents of students who need additional time know from the very beginning that their children can have two years to complete this blended first grade, if necessary. This takes the pressure off everyone—students, teachers, and Mom and Dad. There are no high-stakes campaigns to pass "or else," and no end-of-the-year trauma for students who need another year to develop and learn.

Choices outside the public school system

Unfortunately, too many parents still have to cope with public schools that do not yet offer continuous-progress options for students who need an additional year to learn and grow. Under these circumstances, allowing a struggling learner to have an additional year of education in another setting may be a very positive alternative to finding out the hard way whether the student will "sink or swim" at an arbitrarily assigned grade level. Clearly, very careful consideration must be given before making these choices. Consultation with public school officials is usually advisable and may even be required.

An extra year of preschool

High-quality preschools provide young children with a range of developmentally appropriate activities that foster continued growth and learning. In addition, the mixed age levels found in many preschools make it especially easy for developmentally young children to fit in, just as in a multiage class. This sort of environment also tends to make preschool teachers aware of the importance of readiness, as well as adept at working with children who are at different developmental levels. Unfortunately, in most cases this option is only available to financially advantaged parents.

An additional year at home

Some parents may prefer to provide a late bloomer or other struggling learner with home schooling for an additional year. In situations where there is a parent at home every day who has the time, inclination, and understanding to work with a child in this way, it can be a viable alternative, especially now that more materials and support networks have been developed for parents who decide to provide their children's entire education at home. Keep in mind, though, that opportunities to grow and learn with their peers contribute in many ways to children's overall development. And a full staff of well-trained teachers can often provide a struggling student with a wider range of supportive and educational learning experiences than a lone parent.

Dropping out and "stopping out"

When struggling learners who need an additional year to learn and grow do not receive it early in their educational career, they tend to take the time later on. They may repeat a grade in middle school or high school, or flunk out or drop out altogether. They may also obtain their high school diploma but feel the need to take time off before going to college. Some "stop out"—a phrase used to describe students who take a leave of absence while at college. Statistics show that a large number of students do take time off during college, and interestingly enough, the percentage is about the same as the percentage of children found to need extra time when they start elementary school!

Some of these older students may be ready to put the additional learning and growing time to better use now that they are more mature, but too many others are already crippled by negative attitudes, low self-esteem, and poor skills that interfere with their ability to have productive and fulfilling lives. Early intervention in a positive and supportive way can be far more effective than a wait-and-see approach.

Another option (or requirement?)

One other way to obtain an additional year of learning and growing time is to spend a second year in the same grade, completing the curriculum and obtaining mastery of the skills needed to succeed in the years ahead. While this option remains a choice at some schools, at others the push for high standards has led to its becoming a requirement for students who do not pass a high-stakes test. For a variety of reasons, this approach to providing additional learning time warrants its own chapter, which immediately follows this one.

CHAPTER 7

Is It Okay to Correct a Mistake?

re·place (ree-plays) *verb* To provide a student with an additional year of learning and growing time in order for the student to complete a grade and achieve a correct grade placement in school; traditionally known as retaining, repeating a grade, being left back, etc.

Matching a child with the correct grade or program in school is the most important decision adults make about the child's education. And if a student has been placed in the wrong grade or program, adults have a responsibility to correct that mistake, so that a long-lasting, positive change occurs in the student's education and attitude.

If you have determined that a student is overplaced in school and that other means of providing an additional year are unavailable or inappropriate, you should seriously consider replacing the student *this year.* (By that I don't mean you should go out and get a new student; I mean that you should give the student the additional year of learning and growing time sooner rather than later to prevent even more damage from occurring.) And rather than viewing this replacement as the repetition of a grade, everyone involved needs to acknowledge that the student never really finished the required coursework and therefore is taking an additional year to *complete* the grade successfully.

"Oh, if only it were that easy!" Isn't that what you're thinking? "How can I be sure I won't be making a terrible mistake? Doesn't it damage self-esteem? Won't the other kids tease him? Won't he end up like the big kids in the back of the room when I was in school—the ones who were just waiting to drop out?"

These are troubling and serious questions, of course. But these same questions must also be asked about the risk of allowing the student to remain overplaced and unable to meet grade-level standards, so that his or her educational experience continues to be frustrating, negative, and unsuccessful. Perhaps the best answer I can provide to these questions, which is also the answer of many other experienced educators, is that I have seen countless children become happy, confident, successful students once they have taken an additional year to complete a grade. And I have also spoken with a great many parents who wish they had acted sooner to provide their struggling, overplaced learners with the additional year of growing and learning time they truly needed.

As for the risk of dropping out of school, recent research, common sense, and decades of experience make it clear that grade-level retention is not the actual cause of that problem, but rather one more link in a chain that actually started with the various factors that first led a student to start experiencing daily frustration and failure in the classroom. It is these original factors and the resulting experiences that then led to grade-level retention and helped to make the additional year one more unsuccessful and negative school experience, which may then have further motivated the struggling learner to drop out before graduation.

"We know, because we have data from when these children began school, that the ones who are held back in 1st grade have terrible problems to start with...And so, later on, when children who have been retained do not do well, all of that deficit in performance cannot be attributed to that fact that they've been held back."
– Doris R. Entwisle of Johns Hopkins University, quoted in the December 4, 1996 issue of *Education Week.*

Now that we have entered an era of high standards and high-stakes testing, correcting wrong grade placement through grade-level retention early in a student's academic career has become more important than ever. With standardized tests being used to "grade" individual schools and teachers, not just students, there is more pressure on students to "make the grade" than ever before. And in a growing number of states, remaining an overplaced, below-grade student may no longer be an option in the upper grades. Struggling learners who go through years of frustration and heartache in classroom after classroom may suddenly be stopped at the "gatepost" to middle or high school, officially labeled a "failure" at that point, and *then* be required to spend another year toiling in the same grade, at which point needless damage will have been done and a huge amount of time wasted.

Taking an additional year to complete a grade is not the right option for every student, but neither is relying solely on remediation—or just doing nothing and hoping for the best. The parents and educators in a struggling learner's life need to weigh the risks and advantages, and then make the decision that best meets the specific needs of that individual student.

Giving children a second chance at school success

Let me say right off that I am a firm believer in replacing students at any grade level or age, and at any time during the school year. I also believe that replacement can be achieved without harm to the student and without unusual stress. In fact, I have found, as have many other educators, that students often feel a great sense of relief when they are told they will be taking an additional year to complete a grade, because they know they won't have to keep trying to do the impossible.

"Some people fear that holding a child back will hurt his feelings and damage his ego...But what could be worse for his self-esteem than not being able to read or solve problems, and being at the bottom of the class?"
– Louise Bates Ames, Ph.D., in the April, 1994 issue of *Parenting* Magazine.

In addition to the preceding quote, consider these comments from some actual students who took an additional year to complete a grade:
"I know the answers this year. I love feeling that now I am one of the smartest kids in the class."
"The teacher doesn't have to nag me anymore."
"For once, I am the one who can help the other kids. I'm not the one who always needs help."
"Now I have many friends in school."
"This is the first time since I started school that I can do what is expected of me."

Unfortunately, many students in need of this sort of change have been prevented from receiving it, because during the 1990s the same ideological extremists who claimed that all students would catch up with each other in third grade also tried to prohibit all students from ever spending an additional year in the same grade. Their flawed logic and dubious assertions convinced some schools and parents to embrace "social promotion"—simply moving every student up through the grades each year, no matter how little the students had learned and how far below grade level they had fallen. But just as the failure of the watered-down curriculum eventually led to the current emphasis on high standards, the multitude of problems created by social promotion eventually led to grade-level retention becoming widely accepted as a necessary adjunct to high standards.

By 2002, more than two dozen states had officially ended the practice of social promotion. Unfortunately, many of these same states closely linked the use of grade-level retention to high-stakes test scores. More enlightened educators also consider a variety of other factors, including the student's emotional, social, and physical maturity; the student's birth date; I.Q. scores; the attitude of the student and the student's parents; and—because girls tend to develop more rapidly than boys—the student's gender.

Nationwide, the policies and procedures determining when and how retention occurs vary widely. While some schools may want to retain a below-grade student after he or she receives a single failing score on a standardized test, other schools will not retain students unless a very assertive parent absolutely insists on it. Or a school policy may just require the agreement of the parents and teacher. They notify the principal of their decision, so that he or she can revise the school register, and the deed is done.

Once the decision to replace a student has been made, two key factors determine whether the child has a positive or negative reaction to this important event—how the student is told about it, and any other clue the student picks up from parents and teachers.

The wrong way to tell a student about replacement

Research shows that when many older students repeat a grade, their self-esteem is damaged. Along with everything else I believe, I believe these research findings are true. Why? Because in too many cases students are led to believe it was their own fault that they had struggled unsuccessfully in school for many years and then had to be retained.

For example, suppose parents say to a student, "You know we have been telling you for years that you have to pay more attention in school and work harder. Here you are now in fifth grade, and again your work is below grade level. If you don't straighten yourself out, you're going to have to repeat fifth grade."

After this "wonderful heart-to-heart" talk, suppose the student is still unable to meet the requirements for this grade. Then he is told he is going to be left back. If this student is not hurt by this experience, he is a remarkable child who is not going to be hurt by anything done to him in school. The great majority of students in this situation, however, are going to believe there is something wrong with them, are going to blame themselves for failing, and are going to feel stupid.

Another way of handling the situation is a more gently worded message from the school or parents that would go something like this: "We know you have had a difficult time in school for five long years. We have tried to help you in a variety of ways, but for some reason the problems are continuing. We cannot in good conscience pass you on to the next grade. We want you to stay in fifth grade for another year, so you can get back on track. We're sure you will do better in school and be more comfortable next year."

Do you know what the student receiving this message actually thinks and feels?

"You are keeping me back because you think I am stupid! I tried my best, but it wasn't good enough for you. I already did fifth grade, so you shouldn't make me do it again. Deep down, you think I just don't try hard enough. Well, I do. I work just as hard as the other kids, maybe even harder. But the other kids always seem to know more than I do, and I don't understand everything that's being taught. The teacher teaches too fast, and I don't have enough time to get things right.

"No matter how hard I work, it's never good enough for you. I feel like I've been disappointing you ever since I started school. Now you're going to leave me back and let the whole world know that you think I'm no good at school. You know how that makes me feel? It makes me feel so stupid and bad that I hate school, and I never want to go back."

Why does the gentler message still have such a negative effect on the student? The answer is that it still contains an unspoken, underlying (though clear) assumption that the situation is the student's fault. But if the real cause of the student's problems was an incorrect grade placement decision made years earlier, was that really the fault of a little four- or five-year-old who went to school when and where all the grown-ups told him he should?

Believe me when I tell you that a student does not—repeat *not*—have to feel badly about taking an additional year to complete a grade. In fact, students can feel very good about having this opportunity—and very good about themselves once the opportunity arrives.

What makes the difference in how students feel about an additional year of learning and growing time? Obviously, the actual experience has a lot to do with it, but so does the way in which it is presented.

The right way to tell a student about replacement: "The grown-ups made a mistake."

In talking with a student about taking an additional year to complete a grade, it is imperative to include three key elements in the conversation, if you want the student to have the positive attitude that will help create academic success:

1. Make it abundantly clear to the student that the grown-ups in the student's life made a mistake when they unknowingly allowed a young child to be placed in the wrong grade or program—one for which he or she was not ready.

2. Enlist the student's aid in correcting this unfortunate mistake and helping to set things right.

3. Make it clear that there is now agreement among the most important grown-ups (parents, teacher, and principal) that an additional year of learning and growing time is in the student's best interest. And make sure the student understands that he or she has the whole-hearted support of all these adults.

I would suggest that when parents sit down to talk to a student about taking an additional year to complete a grade, they say something like this:

"Son, I know that school has not been easy for you, this year and in the past. Recently, Mom and Dad attended a meeting at the school, and we heard some new ideas and information that made us think again about some of the earlier decisions we made. After talking it over, we now realize why school is so difficult for you and why the problem is really not your fault.

"For all these years, you've been assigned to the wrong grade. When you started going to school, you really weren't ready for the work in kindergarten. We sent you there because that's what everyone thought we were supposed to do, but now we know better. It wasn't that you weren't smart enough or weren't trying hard, you just needed another year to grow before you were ready to do well.

"It's no wonder that you sometimes felt that you couldn't keep up with the rest of the class and that school was unfair. We used to blame the teachers and the school sometimes, and other times we wondered if we had failed you as parents. We certainly didn't mean to make you feel you were at fault, and now that we know what the problem really is, we can change the situation so that you can start doing better and feeling better.

"We want you to help us correct the mistake that the grown-ups made when you started school. We'd like you to stay with Mrs. Smith for another year and take two years to finish fifth grade. This may be a little difficult at times. The other kids may make some unkind remarks. You will be doing some things over again. But we are sure the benefits will outweigh the problems, or we wouldn't ask you to do this.

"This way you'll have time to learn all the material, so you'll be able to meet the requirements when you go on to sixth grade. We don't want you to continue struggling year after year, and we want you to have time for some fun after school and during vacations. The single most important thing we want is for you to be happy with your life. Please help make this happen by agreeing to stay in fifth grade."

When the matter is outlined to the student in this manner, there's a good chance he or she will feel the burden of guilt start to dissipate. And what a relief it is to be relieved of this burden—to have the heavy weight of four years of failure start to grow lighter. It is especially uplifting when the parents share responsibility. The child actually hears the parents say that they are not perfect and that the child is not to blame.

In addition, this struggling student now knows the real reason school work has been so difficult. It's not a matter of stupidity or lack of effort. School really was unfair, because the student was not yet capable of doing the work successfully. But now that the student can have the additional time needed for growing and learning, he or she will be able to do the work well and succeed in school.

Soon after the parents have this talk with the student, there should be a meeting at which the parents, the student, and the student's teacher are all present. At this meeting, it is helpful for the teacher to say something like the following to the student, while the parents are there listening:

"I am glad you are going to keep working with me in the classroom next year, and I am sure it is the right decision. Looking back from where we are today, I think school would have worked out better if you had spent an additional year in kindergarten or first grade, the way some other students did, but that's all in the past. The important thing is that now we can do something to make the future much better for you.

"I will explain to the class that we have decided you should spend two years in my class. I want you to be my special helper next year. And you won't have to repeat all the work you already understand, because I will have new, challenging materials and activities for you. You will simply begin where you left off. I promise you won't be bored, and I think you'll be pleasantly surprised at how much fun school can be when you don't have to struggle so much of the time. By the time the year's over, you'll feel good about going on to sixth grade."

The student can then feel secure, knowing that his or her parents and teacher are in complete harmony regarding this crucial issue. And presenting grade replacement in this positive way may give the student a sense of stability in regard to school for the very first time. The end result is much more likely to be the sort of change for the better described in the following section.

Three success stories

Peter: Youngest child in the class

"As he stood in the doorway of my classroom, he looked so young and frail. Twenty minutes after he first entered the room, I knew he was in the wrong grade."

Peter's fifth grade teacher saw him for the first time when he transferred to her small rural school from the large city school where he had completed fourth grade. Born during the summer in a state that had a September cut-off date, Peter had always been the youngest child in his class.

The teacher's sense that Peter wasn't ready to meet fifth grade standards was soon confirmed. He didn't understand basic math concepts; he couldn't follow directions; he needed constant approval. Peter wore a path to the teacher's desk, needing to show her how he'd placed his name on a paper, how he'd put in the margins, how he'd numbered each problem. He also seemed anxious about many other aspects of the daily routine. After three weeks of this, the teacher called his parents.

Peter's parents said school had always been a struggle for their boy, even though he was intelligent. Remedial work had helped him keep moving from grade to grade, but it never helped him reach the point where he could do well without it. When the teacher suggested moving Peter to fourth grade, which would be more appropriate for his current stage of development, his parents agreed to discuss the possibility with him. No one was really surprised when even Peter said, "I'm not ready to be in fifth grade."

The next morning, Peter made one more change, moving to fourth grade. And from then on, school work was much easier for him. In addition, his anxiety began to disappear, and he became much happier about his new school and classmates.

Heather: The silent sufferer

When Heather was assigned to a third/fourth grade multiage classroom after a difficult year in second grade, she began to feel overwhelmed by the challenge of doing third grade work and getting along with older classmates. In the spring, the teacher asked

131

the school's principal to observe Heather. As Heather sat in her seat and tried to do multiplication, tears rolled down her cheeks and onto her paper.

The principal arranged a meeting with Heather's parents and teacher, and they discussed the possibility that Heather would benefit from spending another year doing third grade work in the classroom. Everyone agreed that changing the expectations for Heather in the meantime would be a good idea, and then if she needed an additional year, the multiage classroom would be a great place to have it.

By June, Heather was nowhere near completing the third grade curriculum, so when she returned to the classroom the following September, she was able to pick right up where she had left off and still have lots of classmates from the year before in the room with her. While many of those students were doing more advanced work than Heather, she was doing more advanced work than many of the new, younger students. And her teacher was able to manage it all because she was used to working with a range of ages and stages in one classroom.

This time there were no silent tears when Heather worked on her multiplication tables, and even though she had not completed the fourth grade curriculum by the end of the year, she had made new friends among her younger classmates and liked the idea of staying in the classroom with them and her teacher for another year.

The multiage classroom felt very comfortable and familiar during Heather's third year there. She could do fourth grade work successfully, though she had barely scraped by in school up until the prior year. Her previous report cards had portrayed someone in a situation that was not right for her. The side of the report card that reported academic achievement depicted a poor student, while the side that evaluated the person—her work habits, relations with others, ability to take responsibility—described a caring student who tried hard and treated others well.

The opportunity to learn and grow for an additional year made academic success a possibility and then a reality. It also changed Heather from a silent sufferer into a class leader. By the time she reached eighth grade, Heather was a confident, popular student whose name appeared regularly on the honor roll.

Joshua: Better late than never

When Joshua Farrington was in eighth grade, his parents, his teacher, and he himself—after much painful soul searching—decided it would be a good idea for him to take an additional year to complete eighth grade. As Joshua's mother later wrote me, the results made it all worthwhile:

"Another year in eighth grade has made a tremendous difference in Joshua's maturity and readiness for high school. All of his teachers have mentioned the change. Thank you for your part in helping us make this decision. I only wish there had been someone there nine years ago to tell us to wait on entering him in school. It could have spared us all so much pain and frustration."

Joshua summed up his feelings about his experience in the following poem:

I am glad I made the choice
To retain and remain,
And not put so much stress on my brain,
For I am a December boy.
– Joshua Farrington, Grade 8, Vermont.

CHAPTER 8

Same-Grade Solutions for Struggling Learners

Having reached the last chapter of this book, you should now be fully aware of the benefits an additional year of learning and growing time can provide, as well as the many different ways an additional year can be provided. But there still remains the question of how best to help a struggling student in his or her current grade, when effective assistance is needed now.

This may be a student who will receive an additional year to learn and grow next year but cannot just be ignored or abandoned in the meantime. Or this may be a student who is now receiving an additional year and needs a well-structured, individually tailored plan to help put this crucial time to the best possible use.

Additionally, there are and always will be struggling below-grade learners for whom an additional year of learning and growing time is *not* an option—perhaps only at present or possibly forever. Students in these categories might include:
- a student who is already one year older than his or her peers but still needs additional support
- a student trapped in a school that refuses to provide an additional year of learning time under any circumstances
- a student who has a parent adamantly opposed to an additional year of learning and growing time.

Faced with these different possibilities, as well as the many different factors that led these different types of students to become struggling learners, how can you devise a single, easy-to-implement plan that will work for every student?

The answer to this trick question, of course, is that there is no single, easy-to-implement plan that will meet all the needs of the full range of struggling students in today's diverse classrooms. Instead, what you need is a strategy that effectively enables you to use different approaches that meet the different and changing needs of a wide variety of struggling learners. And perhaps not surprisingly, the name now being given to this widely used strategy is *differentiated instruction*.

Making it different makes a big difference

Differentiated instruction is not just a recycled version of previous calls for teachers to "individualize" their curriculum and instruction. That approach, promoted by many of the same people who promised that all students would catch up in third grade and therefore never need an additional year of learning time, did not clearly explain exactly how teachers would meet all their students' individual needs effectively. In contrast, differentiation offers a very clear and effective process for working successfully with students whose work is below grade, at grade level, or above grade level.

The original concept of differentiation was developed by an educator and author named Carol Ann Tomlinson. As the concept has been implemented in schools across America, differentiation itself has been "differentiated" and adapted to meet the needs of diverse educators and students in a wide variety of classroom settings. Following is a brief overview of key steps in the differentiation process that are increasingly being used to help different types and levels of learners in the same classroom:

Assess students first: Rather than waiting until a unit of study is completed, differentiation works best when teachers start assessing students at the *beginning* of a unit, in order to determine the students' current level of knowledge and skills. The teacher can then use the assessment results to identify the level and type of instruction needed by the full range of students in the class, from those who need additional preparation and support to those who need more advanced and challenging work.

Provide "tiered" activities: Knowing the students' differing needs and capabilities, a teacher can then provide appropriate types of curriculum and instruction. Advanced students can have their lessons "compacted," so they do not waste time and grow bored being retaught things they already know. Instead, these students can briefly review a lesson and then move on to more challenging activities that reinforce and extend what they have already learned. Meanwhile, other students who need further preparation and support in order to master a unit can receive materials and instruction geared to their current level, so they make continued progress.

Use flexible grouping: In order to provide students with differing types of materials, instruction, and activities, teachers sometimes need to divide their students into smaller groups based on current capabilities and needs. When used along with whole-class instruction and individual attention, small groups are one more option that allows a teacher to make the most effective use of instructional time. While one group of students works with the teacher to master needed information and skills, other groups can be engaged in tiered activities at the right level for them. And because the groups are temporary and organized around specific subjects or lessons, their makeup can vary and prevent each student from being pigeon-holed as either advanced, average, or below-grade.

Of course, accomplishing all this is far from easy. Educators must first be trained in best practices and then work together to compile and organize their assorted assessments, materials, activities, and techniques. By working together in this way, much of the preparation can be done in advance, making implementation easier and more effective. Then the advantages of this approach quickly become apparent.

First and foremost, by effectively meeting the instructional needs of their full range of students, teachers can spend more time doing what they really want to do — teaching — and less time dealing with all the other problems that arise when students' needs are not being met. Further, effective instruction leads to improved student performance, no small consideration when teachers are under intense pressure to deliver quantifiable results.

However, I believe that differentiating curriculum and instruction is not enough when working with struggling learners whose performance is below grade level. Student support must also be differentiated, and by that I mean not just the provision of support services, but also the use of a student's time before school, after school, on weekends, and during the summer. For with or without a full additional year of school, the amount and use of additional learning time remain key variables that can make a huge difference in a student's performance when they, too, are differentiated.

Time differentiation, when combined with differentiated instruction, results in what I call *differentiation plus*. And to organize all this differentiation effectively for a specific struggling learner, I recommend creating a Differentiation Plus Plan. Like the Individual Education Plan (IEP) required for students who are classified as needing a special education, a Differentiation Plus Plan (DPP) outlines the goals for a specific student as well as the curriculum modifications, instructional accommodations, and additional support designed to help the student achieve those goals.

(See Appendix for models.) Also like an IEP, a DPP should be reviewed periodically to determine how the student is progressing and whether any additional changes are warranted.

A DPP can be created by an individual teacher, but preferably a team approach would be used to create and implement the plan. In today's high-stakes, accountability-driven environment, if a student has been struggling and doing below-grade work for an extended period of time, I recommend alerting the school's principal and requesting assistance in creating an "ad hoc" child-study team. Members of the team could include the principal or an assistant principal, as well as the school psychologist, any relevant specialists, and the current teacher. A previous teacher and a guidance counselor or social worker might also be valuable members. Moreover, a parent's input and participation in the process should always be sought.

The team's first step would be to evaluate the student and review the relevant school records. If additional screening for learning disabilities seems warranted, that should be done right away. Then the plan for modifying the student's curriculum, instruction, and support should be drafted, reviewed, approved, and implemented, with team members continuing to meet periodically to discuss the progress being made and any further modifications that might prove necessary.

Underlying this entire process is a single proposition that educators are increasingly being forced to accept in an era of slogans such as "no excuses" and "leave no child behind." This idea is that if the education we provide does not enable a student to learn well, then we need to provide the type of education that does enable the student to learn well. The next section of this chapter explains in more detail how to do this.

Differentiating what students learn

The implementation of grade-level standards that students and educators are required to meet has resulted in an increasingly standardized curriculum throughout the schools in each state. If each state only had a standardized student population to go along with the curriculum, our school systems would undoubtedly work much more smoothly. But the reality is that America probably has the most diverse student population in the world, and expecting all these different students to learn the exact same material at the exact same time is simply unrealistic. So if the standards represent the destination that all students need to reach, we need to recognize that different students will be traveling different distances and taking different routes in order to reach that same destination.

Differentiating the curriculum is one vital way to help different students complete their educational journeys successfully. While the overall scope and sequence of what the students study remain the same, educators can provide different types of materials to different students—or educators can provide materials that allow students to work in different ways or at different levels. In some subject areas there are already a wealth of alternatives, but differentiating other subjects can prove more challenging.

When it comes to reading, for example, there are numerous series of "leveled readers" for primary grade students. These books are similar in format but have increasingly complex vocabulary and story lines, so one group of students in a classroom can be developing their abilities at one level, while another group is using similar books to develop their abilities at a different level. If a variety of reading levels need to be supported at the middle and high school levels, educators can supplement their standard reading lists with series of "high-low" books that are written at low readability levels but focus on topics of high interest to older students, using formats that do not look "babyish."

140

Writing materials can also make differentiation relatively easy. The use of journals and other open-ended writing materials enables students to work on similar assignments at different levels. These materials can also enable different students to work on topics of particular interest to them, which helps to engage struggling students in the learning process and provides motivation for further effort. "Personal dictionaries" that allow students to include words of their own—or their teacher's—choosing work well for similar reasons, as does the use of spelling lists that mix student-selected words with others designated by a teacher or textbook.

Differentiating math and science is more challenging, although in the elementary grades the use of learning centers can facilitate the process. A well-organized learning center includes a variety of activities and materials that enable students to learn at different levels and in different ways, with guidance and support provided by the teacher. When textbooks become the focus of the curriculum in the upper grades, however, there tends to be less flexibility in regard to the materials. But this is when teachers can have a "menu" of textbook accommodations and extension activities that allow struggling students to continue the learning process at different levels and in different ways. Supplemental nonfiction books at different readability levels can also help, as can computer CD's or web-based materials. And open-ended materials that support "writing across the curriculum" enable students to extend and reinforce their learning, while they also integrate and strengthen important literacy skills.

Social studies presents similar challenges, but similar solutions are available. A single required text may prove difficult for struggling readers to comprehend, but a variety of supplemental texts, whether printed or computerized, may prove easier to understand as well as more interesting. Having a menu of activities that meet different needs and support different interests is also critical, as is the use of "cyber-visits" and other types of electronic exploration.

And open-ended materials that encourage "writing across the curriculum" can prove even more important in this subject area, where extended written responses to test questions become increasingly important.

Overall, the key to making this approach work from an educator's perspective is a process of:
- acquiring a range of materials
- designing or identifying a range of activities and strategies
- organizing the materials and activities effectively
- quickly but continually assessing students to determine their ability levels and areas that need improvement
- providing appropriate guidance and support.

Another vital component, of course, is providing the different types of instruction needed to introduce and support the various types of materials and activities.

Differentiating how students learn

In addition to influencing *what* individual students are taught, differentiation should also be a factor in determining *how* students are taught. The use of varied instructional techniques and strategies can enable struggling students to comprehend and master new information and skills—whereas a rigid and limited instructional style can also prevent some differently able students from learning what they need to know.

Essentially, effective instruction requires consideration and accommodation of two key types of differences found among all types of students:
1. differences in chronological age and/or developmental stage, which help to determine the types of instructional techniques and strategies for which students are currently ready

142

2. differences in students' learning styles, which help to determine how students can best absorb the information that teachers present.

Differentiating instruction for chronological and developmental levels

Responsive educators and parents have long recognized that some techniques work well with younger children but not older ones, and vice versa. That's one reason high school students are treated very differently than primary grade students. But not all educators have been as willing to recognize and acknowledge that significant differences in chronological and developmental levels within a single grade—and even within a single classroom—also require adjustments in the ways information is presented.

Among primary grade students in particular, profound changes in what a student can comprehend may occur rapidly—or not so rapidly. And as the primary grades are a time when students are expected to make the transition from hands-on learning to absorbing abstract information, many primary grade teachers have long used the following three-step process to help students learn:
1. start with something real (have students hold two halves of a sphere and put them together)
2. progress to a realistic representation (show students pictures of two halves that are separate and then two halves put together)
3. end with abstract representation (show students numerical fractions and how they can be added together to form a whole number).

Depending on the chronological and developmental levels of the students in a class, presenting information in a more abstract way may engage many of the older students and leave some of the younger ones totally in the dark. Or focusing too much on hands-on learning may meet the needs of younger students while boring

143

and "turning off" more advanced students. An effective primary grade teacher must therefore use a combination of techniques during whole class activities and then differentiate how—and at what rate—information is presented during small group activities.

In the upper grades, differences in students' levels may be less dramatic but still have a tremendous impact on a struggling learner's ability to succeed. The level of abstraction students can handle and the rate at which they can absorb new information continue to vary widely. At every grade level, educators need to make sure that they are teaching their full range of students effectively, and that the various types of activities used to extend and reinforce learning reflect the different chronological and developmental levels of the students in a class.

Differentiating instruction for learning styles

In addition to different chronological and developmental levels, the students in any class also have varying strengths and weaknesses in regard to the ways they absorb information. Known as learning styles or "modalities," these abilities or tendencies may have physical or environmental causes, or simply be a particular talent or disability that has no clear cause. Whatever their origin, learning styles have long been recognized by educators as a very important component of student learning.

Traditionally, students have been categorized into three basic types of learners:
1. visual learners, who learn best from written or pictorial materials
2. auditory learners, who learn best from spoken or sound-based presentations
3. tactile/kinesthetic learners, who learn best through touch and movement.

In reality, of course, most students learn in all three ways and benefit from having information presented in all three ways. But individual students do have real strengths and weaknesses in regard to these types of learning, and struggling learners are especially vulnerable to having their learning undermined when information is consistently presented in a way they have trouble absorbing. The good news is that identifying and then responding to a student's primary learning style can lead to improved learning and performance.

Visual learners, for example, tend to have an advantage as they proceed through the grades, because an increasing amount of information is presented through books and computer screens. On the other hand, upper grade teachers may tend to lecture their students, which will put a student with weak auditory processing skills at a disadvantage, unless he or she takes very good notes or receives supplemental documentation of what has been said. Highlighting key information, along with other techniques that focus attention on printed material, can be especially helpful for visual learners, as can seating these students where they can see the board clearly and not be distracted by activities occurring outside a window.

Auditory learners, on the other hand, may be able to soak up spoken information like a sponge but then have difficulty absorbing information from a book. Books on tape and "talking flash cards," as well as materials and techniques developed for blind students, can prove very helpful for this type of learner. Auditory learners should also have access to computers and software that are sound-oriented, rather than just the older visually oriented equipment. These students should be seated where they can hear the teacher well and not be distracted by noise from outside the classroom.

Tactile/kinesthetic learners often learn better in the primary grades, where the use of hands-on material and movement activities is more common. In the upper grades, they may need to keep finding ways to use touching and movement to help learn and retain new information and skills. Alternative means of demonstrating what they have learned, such as creating a diorama or acting out a scene, can prove especially helpful for these students.

Of course, educators are most likely to teach their full range of students well by providing a mixture of all three types of learning experiences. But if a student who has trouble learning one way is in a class with a teacher who tends to favor that way of teaching, a list of possible remedies and learning aids should be identified and made part of a DPP. And this same consideration should also be applied to other types of learning styles as well.

In a book entitled *Learning Styles*, author/educator Priscilla Vail also identifies other important learning styles that may be an advantage or disadvantage. For example, she points out that many students learn sequentially, starting with details and working their way up to a conclusion. In contrast, so-called "global thinkers" need to understand the big picture first and then work their way down to the details. Many curriculum materials proceed sequentially, and global thinkers may need to skip ahead to the conclusion before proceeding through the details.

Additionally, some students learn well in three dimensions but have trouble with two-dimensional materials like printed words or numbers on a page. Three-dimensional learners can benefit from working with materials or learning aids that support their perspective, and like tactile/kinesthetic learners, may prove better at demonstrating what they have learned by constructing something or using other three-dimensional means.

Vail also points out that some intelligent, hard-working students have trouble memorizing information or accessing their memories quickly and accurately. As they proceed through the grades, these students may be at an increased disadvantage and have their hard work—or even their intelligence—disparaged, due to a neurological difference that may be beyond their control. The use of mnemonic techniques and aids can prove extremely helpful for these students, as can open-ended, creative demonstrations of learning, as opposed to high-pressure recitations of facts.

Working effectively with these sorts of learning patterns and others, including attention deficts, is also addressed in *A Mind at a Time* by Mel Levine, M.D. He identifies a range of patterns that are neurological in origin, and he recommends creating profiles of struggling learners that will help educators teach more effectively. Howard Gardner's theory of "multiple intelligences" offers another approach to identifying students' individual strengths and weaknesses—and responding accordingly.

Obviously, a complete accommodation of all the different learning styles and levels in a classroom is simply impossible. While a teacher can and should provide an appropriate mixture of curriculum and instruction for her students, very real limits are imposed by state standards, student-teacher ratios, and the amount of time available during the school year. State standards and student-teacher ratios are beyond any individual teacher's or parent's control, but the amount of time a student spends learning during the school year—and how that time is spent—can be modified. This is the third important component of a DPP.

Differentiating students' time

There are many ways in which a student's time can be differentiated, and it would be a huge mistake to look at this crucial variable simply as "time on task." The ugly truth of the matter is that a number of schools have made a big mistake by eliminating recess or reducing lunch time, as well as naps and play time for kindergartners, all in an effort to improve test scores by providing more instructional time. Numerous parents have made similar mistakes by "over-programming" their children with too much tutoring, test-prep courses, and other instructional activities.

An academically extreme approach to the use of students' time is a mistake for two reasons. First and foremost, there are many children, including large numbers of struggling learners, who desperately need more time for creative play, gross-motor activities, and social interaction, in order to handle all the fast-paced, intensive instruction they are already receiving. Just as farmers learned the hard way that they need to leave land fallow at certain times in order to maximize growth at other times, certain administrators and parents will undoubtedly be very surprised to find that children who do not receive an appropriate amount of time off tend to suffer from negative attitudes, physical frustration, and information overload, which then result in *decreased* academic performance.

The second problem with overdoing instructional time is that it often becomes an ineffective substitute for the real solution to below-grade performance. Providing an extra hour per day or day per week or month per year never adds up to a full additional year. Yet administrators or parents who pat themselves on the back for loading up students with an excess of instruction during the school year may steadfastly refuse to provide an entire additional school year to a student who continues struggling despite the smaller amounts of learning time being provided. Obviously, some students only need smaller increments and should not receive a full additional year, but just as obviously, some students need a full additional year because the smaller increments do not suffice and never will.

With that in mind, let's look at the various ways a struggling learner's time can be differentiated to help improve below-grade performance.

Extending support within the school day

Many struggling learners need more specialized assistance and personal attention than a regular classroom teacher has either the training or time to provide. That's why the staff at most schools includes a variety of specialists whose expertise and experience can help small groups of students in need. While the availability of specialists tends to be limited in almost every school, in affluent districts there is usually more monitoring of students and proactive intervention. In poorer neighborhoods there may be greater competition for scarce resources, so assertive advocacy on behalf of a struggling learner may be essential.

With this is mind, careful consideration still needs to be given to the amount and type of support services that will be provided. Students who are constantly being pulled out of class to meet with specialists may feel penalized or stigmatized because they are forced to spend so much time away from their "regular" classmates and teacher. And even a student who is receiving only one support service may still resist it—or view it as a confirmation of his or her inadequacy. That's another reason why a DPP tailored to an individual student's full range of needs is so important.

It's also important because in some schools, a wealth of support services may be available, including time with the following types of specialists:
- reading specialists
- resource teachers
- Title I teachers
- guidance counselors
- school psychologists
- social workers
- speech/language specialists
- physical therapists
- occupational therapists
- ESL teachers

- early intervention specialists
- enrichment specialists.

With some students, therefore, the challenge may be to pick and choose among different specialists in order to make the best possible use of available resources, while also helping the student maintain a reasonable schedule and positive attitude. With other students, the challenge may be to help the student qualify for services and then obtain them, even if this means broadening a definition deliberately kept narrow to exclude students, or finding other ways around tight budgets or bureaucratic barriers.

Extending the school day

Much like time spent with a specialist, an extended school day can be a very positive and effective form of intervention, or it can be a counterproductive burden that makes a struggling learner feel even more hopeless and burnt out. The first consideration, therefore, is how well the following types of options meet the needs of the individual student:

- before-school intervention programs
- after-school intervention programs
- homework "clubs" or similar support at school
- optional after-school enrichment classes
- private tutoring sessions.

Using these types of options to provide additional learning time on a daily basis can help students overcome academic deficits in a supportive environment that also helps to build positive social relationships. In particular, when students need help with one subject, or need access to a place where they can concentrate and receive assistance, or want to pursue an area of interest, extended-day options can provide a vital boost.

The danger lies in "over-programming" struggling learners and creating too long a school day for them, so that they lose motivation, have difficulty concentrating, and resent the loss of opportunities for recreation and socialization. Some struggling learners may desperately need some down time or play time after a tough day in the classroom, in order to "recharge their batteries" or balance negative experiences in school with positive experiences after school. And these days even successful students may find their schedules overloaded with adult-directed, academically oriented activities, thereby missing out on opportunities to develop their creative abilities and social skills.

Extending the school week

Theoretically, Saturday classes, tutoring sessions, or other forms of weekend education sessions can increase a student's instructional time by 20%. As with an extended school day, this can be either a blessing or a curse, depending on the needs of the individual student.

Some students are ready, willing, and able to spend all or part of a Saturday learning, but large portions of their weekends are actually spent in front of a television set instead. Their home environment may be indifferent or even negative toward books and homework. Another possibility is that academic work may be valued, but the language spoken and written at home may not even use the English alphabet, when further exposure to proper English would be of great help to the student. In these sorts of situations, obviously, Saturday sessions can have a very positive impact.

At the other end of the scale, the Saturday schedule for students in affluent areas may already be filled (or overflowing) with enriching activities, including private lessons, sport events, playdates, and family outings. Students in this sort of situation may desperately need some "down time" from all the weekend plans, as well as from the regular school week, especially if they are developmentally young or trapped in the wrong grade for some other reason. After all, there are only about 36 Saturdays in the regular school year,

151

and no one should be fooled into thinking that those days can be an effective substitute for a full year of learning and growing time.

Extending the school year

Summer school or some other form of year-round schooling offers a similar range of advantages and disadvantages. After a traditional summer vacation, the first few months of a new school year are usually a time when information and skills have to be retaught because they were allowed to lapse or totally forgotten during the summer. This is especially true for students who do little or no reading, writing, and arithmetic during the summer and therefore need extra time to regain their good habits and positive momentum. Summer school not only can teach new information and skills, it also can reinforce and extend what students have already learned, resulting in continued progress rather than a go-stop-and-rerun process.

The big mistake lies in thinking that students can do more than two months of learning and growing in just two months. Summer school can solve the problem for students who are just a few months behind, but when students really need a full additional year of learning and growing time in order to complete a grade successfully, two months of summer school will still leave them ten months behind. And when summer school is an inadequate substitute that also deprives students of preferred recreational and educational experiences, the negative attitudes it can engender may make it even less effective.

That's why mandates which require struggling learners to attend summer school are a mixed blessing. What many of those who are forced to attend summer school really needed was an additional year of learning and growing time at the start of their academic career. And that's why the old expression, "an ounce of prevention is worth a pound of cure," applies to education as well as medicine.

Who needs what?

For educators and parents putting together a DPP that includes differentiated curriculum, instruction, and time, the challenge is to mix and match the various possibilities with the specific needs of the individual student. While the critical importance of responding to individual needs limits the value of any general recommendations, the following considerations may prove helpful in creating plans for the key types of students likely to be at risk for below-grade performance. Whenever there is a difference between a specific situation and the general recommendations, however, the specific situation should rule.

Developmentally young students

These students benefit greatly when the curriculum and methods of instruction match their current developmental stage, which may be different than that of many other students in the class. Educators need to remember that many of these students are bright—just younger—and therefore deserve and benefit from extension activities and other challenges at the right level. Remediation and extended instructional time during the school year may not have a positive impact on these students, who really need more time to grow and develop the capabilities needed to meet grade-level standards. However, these students may need social and emotional support, due to the difficulty of relating to more mature classmates and developing a positive self-image.

Impoverished students

The poverty that impacts these students' learning may include a lack of exposure to books, vocabulary, and the world outside their neighborhood. These students therefore need a curriculum and methods of instruction tailored to their current level, along with a rich range of experiences that provide information and other forms of input for which they are ready—and possibly even eager. Extending the school day, week, and year can prove helpful in this regard. These students may also need a wide range of support services, including proper nutrition and medical care, which must be organized and integrated in order to provide effective and appropriate help.

ESL students

These students may be highly intelligent but lack the means of absorbing and expressing information. Overcoming the language barrier is obviously the top priority, and extending the school day, week, and year can help to accelerate and sustain this process. An appropriately balanced curriculum is extremely important, as these students may be capable of working with advanced concepts but still need help learning our alphabet. They may also need basic information about the functional and conceptual aspects of living in the United States, and they may need a range of support services, as well.

Differently able students

These students need carefully tailored instruction in order to master the same curriculum as other students. A variety of support services may also prove necessary in order for these students to succeed, and finding ways to qualify for those services may be a priority. Extended learning time may be less important for these students than social and emotional satisfaction, which can provide the reinforcement and motivation needed to face the challenges that await these students in the classroom.

Putting it all together and wrapping it up

Figuring out what a student needs in order to succeed is not all that difficult. Making it happen is the hard part. As noted earlier, solving major issues, such as obtaining adequate funding for a school or district, may be beyond any individual's control. But parents and educators can work together effectively to provide a specific struggling student with the type of education and amount of learning time that the student needs. That's where change and progress can occur—and make a huge difference.

So start with the individual student and start early. But most of all start now.

Differentiation Plus Plan (DPP)

Student _____ Date of Birth _____
                Name

Present Grade Placement _____ Date _____

Placement Recommendation (grade level/program) _____

School _____ Phone _____

Parent(s)/Guardian(s) _____
                                 Name(s)

Mailing Address _____ Phone _____

Classroom Teacher(s) _____

Notes:

Differentiation Plus Plan (DPP)

Student_____ Date _____

Curriculum Modifications

Goal:_____ _____ Modifications:_____ _____ _____ _____ _____ _____ _____ _____	**Progress Review** Date:_____ Comments:_____ _____ _____ _____ _____ _____ _____
Goal:_____ _____ Modifications:_____ _____ _____ _____ _____ _____ _____ _____	**Progress Review** Date:_____ Comments:_____ _____ _____ _____ _____ _____ _____
Goal:_____ _____ Modifications:_____ _____ _____ _____ _____ _____ _____	**Progress Review** Date:_____ Comments:_____ _____ _____ _____ _____ _____

Differentiation Plus Plan (DPP)

Student_____ Date _____

Instructional Accommodations

Goal:_____	**Progress Review**
_____	Date:_____
Accommodations:_____	Comments:_____
_____	_____
_____	_____
_____	_____
_____	_____
_____	_____
_____	_____
_____	

Goal:_____	**Progress Review**
_____	Date:_____
Accommodations:_____	Comments:_____
_____	_____
_____	_____
_____	_____
_____	_____
_____	_____
_____	_____
_____	

Goal:_____	**Progress Review**
_____	Date:_____
Accommodations:_____	Comments:_____
_____	_____
_____	_____
_____	_____
_____	_____
_____	_____
_____	_____

Differentiation Plus Plan (DPP)

Student_____ Date _____

Additional Intervention Programs and Services

Goal:_____	**Progress Review**
_____	Date:_____
Intervention/Services:_____	Comments:_____
_____	_____
_____	_____
_____	_____
_____	_____
_____	_____
Implemented by:_____	_____
Title/Role:_____	_____
Goal:_____	**Progress Review**
_____	Date:_____
Intervention/Services:_____	Comments:_____
_____	_____
_____	_____
_____	_____
_____	_____
_____	_____
Implemented by:_____	_____
Title/Role:_____	_____
Goal:_____	**Progress Review**
_____	Date:_____
Intervention/Services:_____	Comments:_____
_____	_____
_____	_____
_____	_____
_____	_____
_____	_____
Implemented by:_____	_____
Title/Role:_____	_____

Differentiation Plus Plan (DPP)

Student_____ Date _____

Differentiating Additional Learning Time

- **Before/After School Program**

  _____

  _____

  _____

- **Summer School**

  _____

  _____

  _____

- **Grade Level Completion (Retention In-grade)**

  _____

  _____

  _____

- **Transitional Classroom**

  _____

  _____

  _____

- **Looping/Multiage Classroom**

  _____

  _____

  _____

- **Other Time Options**

  _____

  _____

Boyer, Ernest. *Ready to Learn*. Princeton, NJ: Carnegie Foundation for the Advancement of Teaching.

Brazelton, T. Berry, and Stanley I. Greenspan. *The Irreducible Needs of Children*. Cambridge, MA: Perseus Publishing, 2000.

Brazelton, T. Berry. *Touchpoints*. New York, NY: Addison-Wesley, 1992.

Coletta, Anthony. *What's Best For Kids*. Rosemont, NJ: Modern Learning Press, 1991.

Elkind, David. *The Hurried Child*. Reading, MA: Addison-Wesley, 1981.

Elkind, David. *Miseducation*. New York: Alfred Knopf, 1988.

Elkind, David. *Reinventing Childhood*. Rosemont, NJ: Modern Learning Press, 1998.

Forsten, Char, Jim Grant, and Betty Hollas. *Differentiated Instruction: Different Strategies for Different Learners*. Peterborough, NH: Crystal Springs Books, 2002.

Forsten, Char, Jim Grant, and Irv Richardson. *The Looping Evaluation Book*. Peterborough, NH: Crystal Springs Books, 1999.

Forsten, Char, Jim Grant, Bob Johnson, and Irv Richardson. *Looping Q&A: 72 Practical Answers to Your Most Pressing Questions*. Peterborough, NH: Crystal Springs Books, 1999

George, Paul. *How to Untrack Your School*. Alexandria, VA: Association for Supervision and Curriculum Development, 1992.

Goodman, Gretchen. *Inclusive Classrooms from A to Z: A Handbook for Teachers*. Columbus, OH: Teacher's Publishing Group: 1994.

Grant, Jim. *Developmental Education in an Era of High Standards*. Rosemont, NJ: Modern Learning Press, 1998.

Grant, Jim. *Retention & Its Prevention*. Rosemont, NJ: Modern Learning Press, 1997.

Grant, Jim and Johnson, Bob. *A Common Sense Guide to Multiage Practices*. Columbus, OH: Teachers' Publishing Group, 1994.

Grant, Jim, Bob Johnson, and Irv Richardson. *Multiage Q&A: 101 Practical Answers to Your Most Pressing Questions*. Peterborough, NH: Crystal Springs Books, 1995.

Grant, Jim and Bob Johnson. *Kindergarten Readiness Checklist*. Peterborough, NH: Crystal Springs Books, 1997.

Grant, Jim and Bob Johnson. *First Grade Readiness Checklist*. Peterborough, NH: Crystal Springs Books, 1997.

Grant, Jim and Irv Richardson. *The Retention/Promotion Checklist*. Peterborough, NH: Crystal Springs Books, 1998.

Grant, Jim, Bob Johnson, and Irv Richardson. *The Looping Handbook: Teachers and Students Progressing Together*. Peterborough, NH: Crystal Springs Books, 1997.

Healy, Jane. *Endangered Minds*. New York: Simon & Schuster, 1990.

Healy, Jane M. *Failure to Connect*. New York: Simon and Schuster, 1998.

Keshner, Judy. *Starting School*. Rosemont, NJ: Modern Learning Press, 1992.

Kraus, Robert. *Leo the Late Bloomer*. New York: Windmill Books, 1981.

National Association of Elementary School Principals. *Early Childhood Education and the Elementary School Principal*. Alexandria, VA.

Uphoff, James. *School Readiness and Transition Programs: Real Facts from Real Schools*. Rosemont, NJ: Modern Learning Press, 1991.

Uphoff, James. *Summer Children*. Middletown, OH: J&J Publishing, 1986.

Vail, Priscilla. *About Dyslexia*. Rosemont, NJ: Modern Learning Press, 1990.

Vail, Priscilla. *Common Ground: Whole Language and Phonics Working Together*. Rosemont, NJ: Modern Learning Press, 1991.

Vail, Priscilla. *Emotion: The On/Off Switch For Learning*. Rosemont, NJ: Modern Learning Press, 1994.

Vail, Priscilla. *Learning Styles*. Rosemont, NJ: Modern Learning Press, 1992.

Winn, Marie. *Children Without Childhood*. New York: Penguin Books, 1983.

A

additional learning time 16, 17, 18, 19, 25, 110-119, 121-125, 138, 147-152
after school 16, 27, 43, 46, 51, 62, 150-151
assessment 4, 7, 14, 34, 42, 87, 99, 100, 137, 138
attention deficit disorder 6, 12, 60, 62

B

boredom 67, 72, 130, 137
boys 11, 12, 106, 125
brain 12, 21, 65, 88, 96, 97, 108, 133
Brazelton, T. Berry 87, 98

C

chronological age 8, 21, 22, 45, 54, 88, 89, 142
Coletta, Anthony 11, 27, 33, 112
college 11, 22, 30, 86, 105, 107, 118
counseling 27
covert stress signs 66
curriculum 2, 4, 6-8, 10, 15, 17, 18, 24, 26, 27, 30, 37, 40, 43, 46, 49, 58, 60,
    92, 93, 95, 97, 98, 101, 102, 103, 107-111, 113-116, 119, 124, 132, 136-
    142, 146, 147, 153, 154
cut-off date 2, 8, 30, 35, 54, 89, 131

D

developmental assessment 99, 100
developmental readiness 31, 46, 99, 100-103, 106
developmental stage 7, 8, 9, 30, 45, 58, 88, 89, 90, 91, 93, 94, 99, 142, 153
developmentally young 7, 22, 41, 43, 63, 89, 107, 109, 118, 151, 153
differentiated instruction 43, 136, 138

E

emotional stress 13, 63-64

F

failure 1-9, 11, 13, 15, 16, 17, 18, 19, 21-30, 33, 35, 40, 46, 53, 84, 90, 91, 93-
    95, 97, 101, 104, 107-111, 113, 114, 116, 122-129
first grade 5, 10, 21, 29, 36-41, 62, 91, 96, 98, 105-109, 115, 117, 130

G

Gardner, Howard 147
Gesell, Arnold 100
gifted 22, 33, 100, 105

Quarter Past September
Jim Grant

When it's quarter past September
It's a magic time of life.

The school world of our children
Should be free of strife.

Our little people have waited and waited...
And waited for this day, only to
Learn that school is not
A place for play.

The teacher welcomes one and all
And asks them to sit still,
Most of the children are quick to comply,
Except for overplaced Bill.

The children were given their phonics
Lesson and asked to complete the job,
Everyone finished all their work,
Except for overplaced Bob.

The painters were careful with
The paint—the teachers said "Don't spill."
And all the painters got the message,
Except for overplaced Jill.

At recess time a reminder
Came not to run and race:
No one forget this simple rule,
Except for overplaced Grace.

At the Halloween party, the
Teacher cautioned, "Please don't
Spill your juice," and everyone was
Careful, except overplaced Bruce.

They love their big new pencils,
They love the color red.
Everyone knows the correct way to hold
Them, except for overplaced Ed.

The list of children overplaced is
All a too familiar case.

Shouldn't we watch for signals
And signs that children give
Off when they need more time.

Parent pressure—state law, too,
Send us youngsters before they're due.

High content curriculum we must abide,
But children keep falling by the wayside.

One hundred years from today,
What difference does age make, we'll say.

St. Peter won't stop you at the pearly gate
To ask your age when you graduate.

So many children in their prime
Desperately need additional time.

Let's make school a place to succeed
And give our children the time they need.